T0196426

GOD
MATTERS

The Importance of Belief in a World of Doubt

TIM FRISCH

WESTBOW°
PRESS
A DIVISION OF THOMAS NELSON
& ZONDERVAN

WestBow Press books may be ordered through booksellers or by contacting:

WestBow Press
A Division of Thomas Nelson & Zondervan
1663 Liberty Drive
Bloomington, IN 47403
www.westbowpress.com
1 (866) 928-1240

Because of the dynamic nature of the Internet, any web addresses or
links contained in this book may have changed since publication and
may no longer be valid. The views expressed in this work are solely those
of the author and do not necessarily reflect the views of the publisher,
and the publisher hereby disclaims any responsibility for them.

Any people depicted in stock imagery provided by Thinkstock are models,
and such images are being used for illustrative purposes only.
Certain stock imagery © Thinkstock.

ISBN: 978-1-4908-6180-7 (sc)
ISBN: 978-1-4908-6181-4 (hc)
ISBN: 978-1-4908-6182-1 (e)

Library of Congress Control Number: 2014921251

Printed in the United States of America.

WestBow Press rev. date: 12/9/2014

CONTENTS

PREFACE

My Apologies

An apology can mean a couple of things. Often it refers to saying sorry for something. This is the most common usage in everyday language. However, it can also refer to giving a defense, as in a person giving a defense for his or her beliefs. I would actually like to offer both kinds of apologies here.

First, I would like to say sorry about something. I admit I first wrote the manuscript when I was in my mid-twenties. I am ten years older now, and I am sure that if I wrote it today, it would be an amazing book, much more compelling and insightful than what the reader is about to encounter. Actually, I am just kidding. No book I write is bound to be incredibly noteworthy, because I am not a professional, highly experienced writer. I am being serious when I say that this book is written by an amateur author, so I ask the reader to forgive some of the amateurism that may be displayed in the following pages.

I originally came up with the concept and title of this book while at a store where I saw a bookstand covered with a book titled *Self Matters.* It may seem strange, but I was greatly bothered by the implication of this title and immediately thought there ought to be a book called *God Matters.* (It turns out there are books with this title, but they have a different purpose than that set forth in this book.) And so, not long afterward, I began working on my first book—this volume. It has been ten years since I first began writing it, and to be honest, the reason it has taken so long for me to publish it is not because I have been finely crafting a masterful piece of literature with tireless, laborious effort over the years but because I set it aside after finishing it and kind of forgot about it. I really was not sure it was worth being published. It does convey thoughts gathered from study and reflection on works by great Christian authors such as C. S. Lewis and Ravi Zacharias. In the end, it is largely a reflection of my post-college, early ministry thoughts on Christianity in relation to culture.

While the manuscript lay untouched over the years, there have been times when I thought a volume like this might be useful, and last year I finally decided to take the plunge and have it published. I have since repeatedly gone over the manuscript to try to bring it to the highest standard I am presently capable of producing, but it is still the work of an amateur author. On a good note, an amateur literally means someone who does something for the love of it, and I can say that this book is on a topic I love writing about. I hope the reader will look past my writing weaknesses and try to appreciate the content for what it is.

Now on to my second apology, wherein I offer a defense of or a reason for the content of the book itself. Why write a book on the subject of God? Well, ten years ago I felt that we were living in a time of great skepticism concerning spiritual matters, but now I would say the atmosphere has actually veered toward antagonism. This is especially evident in the literature produced by what have been coined the New Atheists, such as Richard Dawkins, Sam Harris, and the late Christopher Hitchens. These atheists are not only doubtful about God's existence but are also downright aggressive against religious belief systems. So with the resulting antireligious movement that has increased in momentum and influence over the past decade, it makes the subject of this book all the more relevant, and as I went back through the manuscript, I have tried to address some of the issues specifically raised by the New Atheism.

I have also noticed an increasingly negative portrayal of Christianity in much of culture, and I believe it is important for Christians themselves to take the opportunity to explain themselves rather than leaving the explanation of Christianity up to those who either do not believe it or are even opposed to it. The reader will note that this book is written by a believer in God and in Jesus Christ and is meant to convey how I, as one particular Christian, look at the world.

Now comes the point as to whether this book will convince other people to believe. Well, I do not believe arguments are the sole basis for leading a person to faith, but arguments do help people evaluate the merits of their own beliefs and to consider the merits of another viewpoint. So perhaps this book will be an aid in helping some to seriously consider a viewpoint different than their own. But I also hope more directly that this material will help professing Christians to take their own beliefs seriously. This is for their own spiritual encouragement and well-being and also for the good of the Christian testimony in an increasingly antireligious setting. It is important for our culture to observe Christians who not only profess faith in Christ but in whom faith in Christ makes an observable difference. This, more than my book, is probably the best apologetic for Christianity, and my hope is that readers will be influenced beyond thought about God to actually live out their faith in God so others will see that God does in fact matter.

So these are my apologies for this book. If these thoughts have not dissuaded the reader from wanting to read this volume, then by all means, read on!

PART 1

DOES ANYTHING REALLY MATTER?

CHAPTER 1

A QUESTION OF IMPORTANCE

My parents have told me that when I was young, I once told a woman in our church, "You're fat." But apparently in an attempt to soften the harshness of the statement, I went on to console her, "But you're not as fat as your husband." Children are interesting creatures. One thing I find fascinating is that from the simplicity of children come some of the most perplexing questions about life, and sometimes the only answer one can give is, "Now that is a good question." These guileless ones ask questions that all of us deem worthy of consideration, such as: What is time? Why can't people leave each other alone? Where did the world come from? (Or as one of my own young children asked, "How does Darth Vader go to the bathroom?") These are, as we say, good questions because they bring up perplexities that we feel a very strong desire to resolve in our minds.

So to introduce the subject of this book, I have a good question: "Does anything really matter?" Or to state it more precisely, "Does anything truly, inherently, or actually matter in the context of the reality in which we live?" At first this may appear hard, if not impossible to answer, at least in an objective sense. In reality, though, the question itself alludes to an answer because it implies the answer matters, which is why the question is being asked in the first place. In fact, all good questions, including this one, assume there is some issue that actually matters. If nothing truly mattered, there would really be no reason to ask questions in the first place. Therefore, the fact that people ask questions and we think they are good enough to be pondered implies that certain things do indeed matter.

It may seem to some that my answer is insufficient, and I do intend to show more extensively why I believe certain things about life truly do matter. However, at the outset it needs to be pointed out that it is contradictory to make any argument against this proposition because to argue that nothing truly matters assumes that the issue itself matters enough to merit an argument against it.

This is what is puzzling about people who claim there is no transcendent purpose or inherent meaning to life. They spend so much time trying to prove their point as if it really matters. But if there is no ultimate meaning to life and nothing ultimately matters, then there is no reason to try to prove anything. So from their standpoint, there is really nothing worth arguing about.

The fact is, however, everyone cares about certain things, even people who think life has no inherent meaning or purpose. That, after all, is why they argue; they care about what they and others believe. But here again, the word *care* would have no meaning if nothing truly mattered. I care about my wife and children because they matter to me. People care about their houses, money, food, health, and so on because these things truly matter to them. You are reading this book probably because you care about finding out what I have to say. (Then again, you may already be losing interest in what I am saying because you really *don't* care.)

The Age of Skepticism

I have brought up this question of whether anything really matters because it seems that many people have become skeptical about life and its meaning. My conversations with others have led me to believe many people would like to find answers to deep questions about life, but because of the pervading mind-set of our time, they have come to the conclusion that these questions can never be answered with any sufficient level of certainty.

Our time in history is unique, particularly because of the surge in scientific discovery and technology over the past few hundred years. Scientific progress has accomplished much for humanity by uncovering the intricacies of the world in which we live, utilizing this knowledge to develop some of the most incredible devices ever conceived and devising means with which to help people to live longer, healthier lives. I am most respectful and grateful toward science and the advances that been accomplished through it.

There is a downside to all of this, however. Our scientific mind-set has led us to believe we can only be sure about certain things, namely anything that is scientifically explainable. People tend to be sure only about the things endorsed by mainstream science and often rely upon scientific verification before they will accept something as fact. This leads them to believe it is impossible to know the factuality concerning nonphysical (i.e., spiritual) matters. A person's faith, therefore, is simply a matter of opinion, and there is no way to know the truth about matters outside the physical, observable realm of life because science is unable to prove it. As a result, people often believe a person must separate science and faith—that they do not coincide. Science, therefore, is considered something to be universally accepted as fact, whereas religious beliefs are considered something to be personally accepted as opinion.

I have two responses about this mind-set. The first is to point out that there are many things people know to be true that science is simply unable to explain or prove. I remember watching a TV show called *More Than Human*. It showed people with some unusual and amazing abilities. For example, it showed a man capable of withstanding a bed of nails pressed up against his back under extreme pressure without injury, and another man who could take a kick in the groin without flinching. I'm not sure how or why these men discovered they had these abilities in the first place (one has to wonder), but I'll never forget the response of the doctor they interviewed on that show. He said there is nothing in his Western medical understanding of the human body that could explain these abilities. The fact is that science is not able to account for every phenomenon that is a part of the reality of our world, so people must not become so dependent upon it that they fail to recognize its shortcomings. It is possible to know the factuality of certain things even if science is unable to explain or prove them.

Second, it might be tempting to ask, "Why do we need to figure out anything outside of the realm of science? Why not just give up arguing about religion and matters of faith and just enjoy life?" The problem here is that when life is approached from a merely physical perspective, it becomes increasingly difficult to enjoy over time. American society is a good example of this. As there has been an increase in agnosticism concerning matters of faith, there has been an increase in discontentment, despair, emotional disorders, and other social ills.

The reason for this phenomenon, I believe, is that in order to enjoy life to the fullest, people must live with a true sense of purpose and have values to guide them. Unfortunately, science alone does not provide the groundwork for this. One might tell people they ought to treat each other well (which is a moral principle), but there is no absolute reason for doing so without a certain belief that goes beyond the realm of science. One may also try to tell people they are special and that their lives do have purpose, but science gives no concrete reason to believe this.

While it is true many agnostics and atheists do, in fact, seek to live moral lives and feel they have a purpose, the point I am making is that there is no scientific basis for holding to these notions. They are simply choosing to live that way apart from any reason provided by their worldview, and this lays the groundwork for serious problems.

When author Philip Yancey visited Russia in 1991 after the collapse of atheistic communism, he spoke with the editors of the communist publication *Pravda*. He recounts,

> The authors remarked wistfully that Christianity and communism have many of the same ideals: equality, sharing, justice, and racial harmony. Yet they had to admit the Marxist pursuit of the vision had produced the worst nightmares the world has ever seen. Why?
>
> "We don't know how to motivate people to show compassion," said the editor-in-chief. "We tried raising money for the children of Chernobyl, but the average Russian citizen would rather spend his money on drink. How do you reform and motivate people? How do you get them to be good?"[1]

So one problem is that a purely material-based philosophy provides no basis or impetus for doing what is good. Additionally, it

---

[1]   Philip Yancey, *The Jesus I Never Knew* (Grand Rapids, MI: Zondervan, 1995), 75.

fails to provide a sufficient guard from engaging in what is wrong. There are many times when it is personally advantageous and self-gratifying to do something unethical, such as lying or stealing in order to gain financially. As long as no one is really hurt by this behavior, there is no scientifically based reason to abstain from doing so.

Furthermore, history has shown that when people have no sense of accountability beyond the physical realm, the door to increasingly corrupt behavior can open. A graphic example is seen in an account given by the late Romanian pastor Richard Wurmbrand, who was brutally persecuted under an atheistic regime. Commenting from personal experience, he writes,

> The cruelty of atheism is hard to believe. When a man has no faith in the reward of good or the punishment of evil, there is no reason to be human. There is no restraint from the depths of evil that is in man. The Communist torturers often said, "There is no God, no hereafter, no punishment for evil. We can do what we wish." I heard one torturer say, "I thank God, in whom I don't believe, that I have lived to this hour when I can express all the evil within my heart." He expressed it in unbelievable brutality and torture inflicted on prisoners.[2]

Again, I readily admit that atheism does not automatically lead to this kind of situation, but denying the spiritual realm does present a logical framework in which all sorts of destructive behavior can

---

[2] Richard Wurmbrand, *Tortured for Christ* (Bartlesville, OK: Living Sacrifice Book Co., 1967, 1998), 36.

thrive and be justified, and history has amply proven this to be a potential threat.[3] It must be recognized, therefore, that there is a danger in seeking to have a society that only acknowledges the physical world. Letting science alone guide a culture's philosophical viewpoint and values does not provide a sufficient foundation for a peaceful, safe, and happy society.

So it appears that the situation is at an impasse. On one hand, it seems impossible (based on the scientific method alone) to know for certain the truth about matters of faith, meaning, and morality. But on the other hand, if society does not have a system that provides the moral groundwork and purpose for people's lives, then people will continue to have to deal with the dangers and consequences of a life confined to the physical, scientifically provable realm. American culture, in spite of those who put a good face on it, is facing the turmoil of this very situation.

The Common Belief

I believe the answer to this dilemma may be found by examining a fact I have already commented on. Though humans may disagree about many different things, all share a common belief. It is a belief that goes beyond the reach of science and penetrates a realm of life that, though it is not physical, is just as real and knowable as the material world in which we live. I am referring to the inherent belief that certain things in life matter.

---

3   Later on we will discuss the use of religion to justify evil actions, but the point here is that naturalistic atheism has indeed provided the groundwork in which to engage in morally reprehensible behavior, in spite of those who would argue to the contrary.

This belief is so imbedded in human nature that it comes out in many facets of our lives. It is what causes us to discuss issues. We carry on conversations every day that are filled with ideas, individuals, and circumstances that matter deeply to us. In some cases, we even argue over these ideas, as observed in political and religious discussions. (Where would cable news be if it weren't for this propensity?) Probably some will argue against the ideas proposed in this book, and the reason they will do so is because they believe these issues matter.

Our belief in what matters is also witnessed by our sense of pain. We question why we have to face sadness, hardships, the death of loved ones, and so on because these things matter to us. We try desperately to heal this pain by looking to medicine, books, religion, or anything we can get our hands on that will help us to deal with problems that matter to the core of our being.

Then there are our works of creativity. Every song that is sung, book that is written, or movie that is produced contains elements of the issues that matter to our lives, which is why we create and enjoy them in the first place. The universal fascination with a story like *Les Misérables* is a testimony to this. It has been adapted to the stage and screen and has met with enormous success as countless people identify with the themes contained in this work, such as love, justice, tragedy, redemption, fighting against oppression, and seeking a world of true peace. One of the musical version's creators said that when people hear the final song, "Do You Hear the People Sing?" which is sung to the audience, people respond passionately with agreement to the call to stand for what will bring a better world, even though they may have no clue how to do so.[4] The human heart

---

[4]   *The Story of Musicals,* BBC Presentation.

clearly resonates with certain ideals, and there is a deep-felt response in all of us, indicating a belief that certain things truly do matter.

A Reason for Optimism

I see in all of this a reason for hope. All people share a common belief, the hint of truth that lies at the bottom of every one of our souls. In the end, we are not the skeptics that we claim to be, for we actually do possess a very strong belief that reaches beyond the realm of science. We do not have to live in a world of doubt and despair after all!

Our feelings and behavior are indicators of knowledge that humans possess about something that cannot be seen or scientifically explained. There was a man I used to work with who had no religious beliefs, but when he faced situations such as someone treating him unfairly, he would become angry because he believed that person's behavior was wrong even though he had no specific basis on which to make that assessment. He believed in something—a value, a principle—that could not be identified scientifically but that he felt should be applied to every person. Even the modern, outspoken writers of the New Atheism exemplify this attribute in their continual appeal to moral standards as a prime basis for their arguments.

The way people feel and behave in relation to one another might be likened to being in a football game. There are certain rules or expectations, and there are certain actions that take place in a football game solely because of the contextual reality of the game itself. I would not walk up to someone in a grocery store and shout, "Delay of game!" (though it might be tempting to do so when standing in a long line) because there is no such thing as delay of game outside of the context of a football game. One would think I were quite strange if we were walking down the street together, and I suddenly yelled, "Blitz!" and tackled a person coming the other way. These things are perfectly acceptable and even expected in a football game, but outside of that context, it would not make sense to behave in that way. In the same manner, the attitudes and rules people have about life indicate that there is some sort of a game, so to speak, that all of us are a part of and know about.

More specifically, if certain things really do matter, which all humans show evidence of believing, then there must be a reality that people are assuming as the basis for which everything matters, a contextual paradigm that is beyond the realm of scientifically provable data. It is the subject of this reality to which I will give attention next.

CHAPTER 2

WHAT MATTERS MOST

I would now like to build on what has been established so far. It has been observed that there is a universal notion that certain things in life truly matter. This notion indicates a contextual paradigm that exists beyond the realm of what is scientifically observable. It is what may be called the reality of the transcendent. I want to go further now and propose that our natural views of life are best explained by the existence of a supernatural entity (i.e., the being of God).

If there is nothing beyond the physical realm, then there is really no transcendent purpose to the universe, and if there is no purpose, then in the end all is pointless and nothing ultimately matters. And if this is the case, then all of the standards, expectations, and values we have are without a basis. Thinking back to the football game analogy, one can, and people often do, complain about the behavior of others. There are rules to which we all hold each other accountable. But someone can't break a rule of football unless he is in the context of a football game. In the same way, one can't break a rule of life or a moral standard unless there is a game or purpose to life, which is the context for those rules, and without a transcendent purpose-giver, there is no overarching, true purpose behind everything.

This is a great dilemma for our society because people try to separate their beliefs about the supernatural from their ideas of morality. But herein lies a serious problem: without the existence of a supernatural entity, not only is there no objective basis for morality or rules (because life has no objective meaning or purpose), but there is also no objective way of determining which rules to follow. The popular answer to this is for each person to make up his or her own rules, or to do what you feel is right for you. Ironically, however, people turn around and revert back to their belief in a universal standard the moment someone does something they believe is truly wrong. While Americans may preach tolerance, there are people on both sides of every issue acting as if all people should live up to the standards they are presenting. And people in our society will even judge other societies (such as the Nazi society) based on a universally applied standard, which they supposedly do not believe in.

For instance, I once had a discussion with a man who said people should be able to decide what is right for themselves and that certain things may be wrong for certain people but not others. In other words, "Do what is right for you." I asked him how he would respond if I thought it would be all right to kill his mother, to which he replied, "I'd kill you if you did that!" He would thus hold me accountable for what I did. But his response belies a contradiction to what he had previously stated, for now he was holding me to *his* standard of morality which says, "Don't kill an innocent person."

C. S. Lewis, the well-known author who was once an atheist, associates this universal morality with the concept of the supernatural.

My argument against God was that the universe seemed so cruel and unjust. But how had I got this idea of *just* and *unjust?* A man does not call a line crooked unless he has some idea of a straight line. What was I comparing this universe with when I called it unjust? If the whole show was bad and senseless from A to Z, so to speak, why did I, who was supposed to be part of the show, find myself in such violent reaction against it?… Of course, I could have given up my idea of justice by saying it was nothing but a private idea of my own. But if I did that, then my argument against God collapsed too —for the argument depended on saying that the world was really unjust, not simply that it did not happen to please my fancies. Thus in the very act of trying to prove that God did not exist—in other words, that the whole of reality was senseless—I found I was forced to assume that one part of reality—namely my idea of justice—was full of sense. Consequently atheism turns out to be too simple.[5]

The fact that all people have rules, or a sense of justice as C. S. Lewis calls it, that they believe in a purpose to life, and that there are certain aspects of life that truly matter all point to a transcendent entity that undergirds how people think and interact. I find it significant that though an increasingly large number of people today argue vehemently against the existence of such a being, humanity

---

[5]   C.S. Lewis, *Mere Christianity* (New York: Harper Collins Publishers, 1952, 2001), 38–39.

still largely embraces the concept. People all over the world engage in some form of worship of a transcendent being or God that they are convinced exists. It seems natural to believe in a higher power that has designed everything. Even children evidence a natural belief in a teleological order or purposeful design to life, as seen in studies conducted by psychologist Margaret Evans of the University of Michigan. Jesse Bering writes,

> Evans has discovered that regardless of their parents' beliefs or whether they attend religious or secular school, when asked where the first member of a particular animal species came from (say, a fox or a turtle), 5- to 7-year-old children give either spontaneous generationist (e.g., "it got born there") or creationist (e.g., "God made it") responses. By 8-10 years of age, however, children from both secular and religious backgrounds give exclusively creationist answers. Typically these answers are manifest as "God made it," but often "Nature" is personified, seen as a deliberate agent that intentionally made the animal. It's only among the oldest children she's studied, the 10-12-year-olds, that Evans uncovers an effect of developmental experience, with children of evolutionary-minded parents giving evolutionary responses and those of evangelical parents giving creationist answers to the question.[6]

---

[6] Jesse Bering, "Creationism Feels Right, but That Doesn't Make it So" (available at http://web3.scientificamerican.com/article. cfm?id=creationism-feels-right-but-that-doesnt-make-it-so; accessed February, 2014).

It is natural for humans to assume a transcendent order, purpose, and design to the universe, and the worldview that gives a consistent basis for these ideas is that there is a transcendent being who has designed the world with purpose.

Why *Can't* We All Just Get Along?

Certainly the question at this point is if there really is a supernatural being (i.e. God) and the truth concerning spiritual matters can be known, then why does not everyone agree on these matters? It needs to be said at the outset that people's lack of agreement does not negate the truth of the matter. If two children are fighting about something and their mother asks what happened, they may give two different stories, but the mother would not assume that there is no factual answer as to what really happened. Instead, it is understood that their answers may be skewed because of personal bias and perception, but as she digs deeper into both of their stories, she begins to find out the underlying facts, which will lead to the truth of the situation.

This is similar to what happens when approaching matters of faith. We must realize that our lack of agreement may have more to do with *us* than with the evidence at hand. There are a few different tendencies people have that can lead to the disagreements often seen concerning God and spiritual matters.

The first is close-mindedness about one's personal views. Sometimes people have a view in their minds that they insist must be right no matter what evidence is given to the contrary. The highly religious are often accused of this, but it is by no means limited to this category, for there are even nonreligious people who are closed-minded about spiritual matters. One does not exactly see open-mindedness, for example, in the works of a nonreligious (actually antireligious) man like Richard Dawkins. This type of mentality obviously keeps people from coming toward agreement because the evidence that would help to clarify the issues is blocked by dogmatic beliefs.

A second tendency is for people to throw out the evidence they do not like. I can think of many people who struggle with their beliefs about God because of painful experiences. I know a family who has had to grapple with the death of their first child. Many people have difficulty coming to terms with the concept of God because of tragic situations like this or simply because in looking at the evidence, they are afraid of the implications, such as a change in lifestyle or rejection of peers. Though these are real challenges, the evidence has to be accepted for what it is, whether we like it or not. Otherwise we will never be able to get to the truth.

A third tendency is to give exclusive authority to personal experience. The problem here is that people can be duped into all kinds of ideas when they solely let experience and intuition guide them. I remember watching a salesman give a presentation at a Wal-Mart one day when I was shopping. He began by saying he would give us all a free knife if we would listen to him speak for a few minutes. Within a short amount of time, he was showing us all of the amazing features of his special knife set. Now no one really needed or wanted this knife set at first, but the more everyone saw the things he could do with those knives (even cutting through a large hunk of metal!), the more they became interested. He also went on to say that he would give several of these knives for one "low" price and even throw in a plastic juicer for free. By this time, people were beginning to actually contemplate buying the knives, and sure enough, they were snagged the moment he said that the first four buyers would receive a free hunting knife. There was nothing really wrong with those individuals being convinced to buy knives, but it is this propensity to be easily swayed by immediate experience without thoroughly examining the facts that causes many people to buy into some things that simply are not true. Humans are highly persuaded by presentation, and this only adds to the confusion concerning matters of spirituality.

Finally, there is a tendency to look at the failures of religion as evidence against God. Some people have been hurt or used by someone who espoused religious beliefs, or they think of atrocities committed in the name of religion. They therefore conclude that religion has been tried and found wanting. What they are overlooking is the fact that in many cases people who commit these crimes are not actually following their religious beliefs. Take, for instance, the massacres committed by the "Christians" of the crusades or the inquisition. They were actually violating and not following the teachings of Christ. Christ never endorsed violence as a means of advancing His kingdom. And people today who hurt others are not following Christ's teachings either. They are going against the very thing they claim to believe, for Jesus teaches that we should love one another. Now while the actions of these people may evoke our ire, they are not proof against spiritual truth. These actions merely reveal that people may claim to believe something but live in contrast to that very belief system. This is no valid proof against the belief system itself.

What If We Ignore the Truth?

There still may be some who feel that I am making a bigger deal out of this concept of truth than I ought to be. It may seem that people can get along just fine without worrying about these issues.

It is becoming more popular today, thanks in part to the efforts of the New Atheists, to claim that spiritual beliefs are actually the cause of all of our problems in the first place, especially the view that one belief system in particular is right. This, they say, is the source of prejudice and hatred toward others. This argument overlooks a few important points, however.

The first is that there are many people with strong spiritual beliefs who clearly possess a great amount of love and concern for others. Many of the great social causes taken up throughout history and even today have been performed not in spite of but *because of* religious beliefs. It is true that religion can be a means of prejudice, but this is not necessarily because of the teachings of the religion itself but rather because of people who twist it into something it was never meant to be. In reality, a religion such as Christianity teaches very plainly that we are to care for those in need and even show kindness toward those who are our enemies. This is certainly not a basis for prejudice and hatred. And many followers of this religion have been moved to great acts of sacrifice and compassion because of their belief in the teachings of Christ. So religion can actually be a catalyst for doing much good.

Second, those who desire to downplay or even eradicate spiritual belief systems (i.e., the nonreligious or antireligious) can also have an exclusive system of their own by which they are essentially judging others and showing prejudice. It is interesting that some of the most antireligious people today are also some of the most outspoken and critical voices in this culture. They do not simply desire for people to cast off religious beliefs but also for the populace to subscribe to their own value system, and those who do not do so are labeled backward and even dangerous to society. Neglecting matters of spirituality does not necessarily lead to a tolerant, open society; it merely creates a vacuum in which new dogmas based on alternate philosophies become the standard by which society operates. Business owners today, for example, are being threatened to lose their franchises if they do not give in to the new ethic, even if it violates their own consciences.

Finally, there is the fact that neglecting to pursue truth has its own negative consequences. One could insist that the truth of "gravity" is too restrictive and decide to ignore it, but it is certain that one will experience some negative effects as a result of this decision, such as when he decides not to bother using stairs from the upper floor. Ignoring the truth has been, in a general sense, our society's response to the problems with spiritual belief systems, but it has raised its own problems that, in the end, may prove to be even greater than the ones it was trying to avoid in the first place.

I have already discussed the idea that, in light of our inherent belief that certain things in life matter, there is a purpose to life and that there are certain rules that we feel everyone ought to follow. There must, therefore, be an underlying basis for these beliefs, which points to the existence of a transcendent entity. Instead of acknowledging this notion, our culture has increasingly replaced this concept with the philosophy of naturalistic humanism (humanity is the measure of all things; the physical is all there is), but just as denying the truth of gravity will have its consequences, so does denying the spiritual truths that undergird our existence.[7]

The tendency for mankind to disregard the truth concerning spiritual matters is nothing new. Two thousand years ago, a follower of Jesus named Paul, a brilliant thinker who sought to persuade others to follow Christ, wrote a letter to the Christians in Rome. It is referred to as the book of Romans in the Bible. In the first chapter

---

[7] J. Budziszewski, in the book *What We Can't Not Know*, argues that the natural moral law has natural consequences that are unavoidable.

of this letter he speaks of people as those who "suppress the truth" and "exchanged the truth about God for a lie" (Romans 1:18, 25). He goes on to speak of the consequence of this choice, which, in essence, is the moral decay of society and the demise of its well-being.

There is evidence today of the very thing Paul is describing all around us. Our choice to suppress the truth is what some people have termed liberation from the uninformed, outdated, restrictive ways of our ancestors. The Christian apologist Ravi Zacharias puts our "liberation" into perspective.

> Is this liberation synonymous with the fact that we have become on one of the most violent and drugged nations on earth? Is this the exhilaration that makes sedatives and antacids the most highly sold drugs across pharmaceutical counters, to slow us down from our mad rush for ever-increasing wealth? Is this the exhilaration that is sending our songwriters and musicians into a frenzy on the stage and into a stupor into their home? Is this the exhilaration venting forth on our talk shows that pride themselves in profane argument as entertainment? Is this the exhilaration that has fragmented our families and often victimized the weakest in our midst? Is this the exhilaration of living in the bloodiest century of history? Is this the exhilaration of a generation of young people often fatherless, many times hopeless? All this reason for exhilaration? Or are we playing deadly word games once again?[8]

---

8   Ravi Zacharias, *Can Man Live Without God?* (Nashville, TN: W Publishing Group), 31.

These descriptions are frighteningly true of our culture, and conditions have only gotten worse in many ways since these words were written. Television shows have become more graphic and degrading. An increasing number of students have taken open fire on their classmates and teachers. Cultural battles have become ever more divisive. And the political system has become increasingly clouded and gridlocked. It is no wonder that self-help books and antidepressants are such popular means of coping with all that is happening. This sounds all too much like Paul's depiction of the continual downward spiral leading toward moral chaos and despair.

Even more alarming is that Paul's portrayal of society is prefaced with the statement that "The wrath of God is being revealed from heaven against all the godlessness and wickedness of people" (Romans 1:18 NIV). Now while at first this may seem absurd and offensive to people who do not particularly believe in the Bible, it is a concept worthy of consideration, for if there were a supernatural being that was truly good, it would make sense for this being to respond with wrath (anger) against what is evil. (We, after all, seem to respond this way toward perceived evil.) Paul is saying that the evidence of God's wrath is that God allows people who deny the truth to do what is wrong and face the consequences of their actions. In the end, society gets what it asks for and becomes imprisoned by its inability to escape from the damage done by the choice to live in neglect of spiritual truth. It is not worth the risk of ignoring and denying the truth about spiritual matters.

Where Hope Lies

Is there any hope, then? And if there is, where can it be found? It is for this very reason that I write these words—to offer hope—but I must add that people should take care not to rest in false hope. What has gotten us into this mess in the first place is neglecting the truth, and this, therefore, is where we must begin.

In this search, one must be willing to do two things. The first is to be willing to accept God as He truly is. Paul lays out the issue in this way: "For since the creation of the world God's invisible qualities—his eternal power and divine nature—have been clearly seen, being understood from what has been made, so that people are without excuse. For although they knew God, they neither glorified him as God nor gave thanks to him" (Romans 1:20–21 NIV). Mankind's greatest problem has never been accepting the idea of the supernatural but embracing the true God—the God who has been revealed in the world around us. Even today many people believe in a god that is palatable to American sensibilities but is not, in fact, the true God. They base their opinions of God on how *they* think God should be. The problem is, this version does not coincide with reality.[9] The fact is, not everyone will initially like everything about the true God; they may even have a very hard time with certain things about this God. So there is a choice. One can either continue to live with an inaccurate view of God (or deny God's existence altogether) or one can follow where the evidence leads and acknowledge God in a way that coincides with reality.

The second thing one must be willing to do is to respond to God in the right manner. Paul says that another problem is that humans are unthankful (Romans 1:21). In other words, not only do they refuse to recognize God as He truly is, but they also refuse to respond correctly to the things He has done for them. The result is wrong ways of thinking and behaving, which is what ultimately

---

[9]   I would agree that some people's perception of God is about as believable as the infamous "flying spaghetti monster" mockingly referred to by many atheists today in their arguments against God.

leads to the downward spiral mentioned previously. Instead of responding to God with gratitude, humans turn toward themselves and seek to live apart from God. This is what is seen more and more in our culture today.

I believe with all my heart that hope for this culture and for individual lives comes by reversing this cycle through pursuing and accepting truth concerning spiritual matters. To this end, the next portion of this book will look at issues that matter to all humans and discuss what they reveal about God and spiritual reality. My desire is to help readers consider the evidence for spiritual truth and the implications of embracing spiritual truth.

PART 2

OTHER MATTERS

CHAPTER 3

THE MIRACLE OF LIFE

I remember like yesterday sitting in an operation room next to my wife. She was having a C-section, and at the nurse's direction, I stood up to look over a curtain to see the doctor take a tiny human being out of my wife's womb. The baby immediately began to make an extremely loud, incessant noise that I would soon become very accustomed to hearing. Before I knew it, the nurses had cleaned the little five-and-a-half-pound "peanut" (as they called it), swaddled it in a blanket, and placed it in my arms. There I was, looking into the tiny face of my first child, Nathanael, who was already sleeping, and then I looked over at my wife, who was also already sleeping. This moment was a miracle.

I have heard people talk about how they would like to be able to witness a miracle, and I would answer by saying they already have, many times. Life itself is a miracle, and many people thus refer to it as such. My son's birth attests to the miraculous nature of life. I remember that though the operating room was filled with various machines and devices of advanced technology, no one was paying attention to those things. Technology may be amazing, but it is not miraculous. The attention of all of the doctors and nurses in that room was riveted by the precious life of that tiny infant, and even though this was probably something that they had witnessed thousands of times before, they all stared in wonder because, once again, they were witnessing a miracle—the miracle of life!

Some take issue with use of the word *miracle*. To them, the birth of a child, the sprouting of a plant, the intricate workings of a single cell, or the vast complexities of the stars and galaxies, though undoubtedly incredible, are simply considered to be natural. This is characteristic of a culture increasingly influenced by a naturalistic philosophy. Others, myself included, feel that this outlook fails to capture the mysterious wonder of the world we live in. G. K. Chesterston wrote, "The only words that ever satisfied me as describing Nature are the terms used in the fairy books, 'charm,' 'spell,' 'enchantment.' They express the arbitrariness of the fact and its mystery. A tree grows fruit because it is a *magic* tree. Water runs downhill because it is bewitched. The sun shines because it is bewitched."[10] But even a naturalistic thinker such as Richard Dawkins speaks of the temptation to see purposeful design in nature and admits a sense of wonder and thankfulness at what he observes in the universe.[11] It appears that even when a naturalistic philosophy is strongly espoused, the human heart cannot help but attest to the miraculous nature of life.

Seeing the miraculous, though, is often clouded by the notion of drawing a dichotomy between science and the supernatural. Science, however, merely shows how things work; it cannot explain how

---

[10]   G.K. Chesterton, *Orthodoxy* (London: William Clowes and Sons, Ltd., 1908, 1934; Kindle Edition), 44–45.

[11]   Richard Dawkins, "Atheism is the New Fundamentalism" (debate sponsored by Intelligence Squared), 2009.

or why they got there in the first place. Science tells us there is a law of gravity, but just because scientists know something about gravity does not explain how it came to be or why it is there. As mathematics professor at Oxford John Lennox points out, scientific laws are descriptive and predictive, not creative—just as the laws of arithmetic describe how money in a bank account will add up but they do not create the money itself.[12] Naturalism ultimately falls short in satisfying questions concerning origin and purpose.

The Source of Life

An increasing number of scientists, picking up on the void left by naturalism, have openly made a connection of their work in relation to the supernatural. For example, Michael Behe, a professor of microbiology at Lehigh University, in his book *Darwin's Black Box* has expressed his belief in a Designer and the inadequacy of trying to explain the development of the microbiological world from a purely naturalistic standpoint. Even though he was extensively trained in the teachings of naturalism, his scientific work continually swayed him to the realization that there had to be a supernatural design involved in the biological workings of living organisms.

His stance, as well as that of other scientists, has not received a welcoming response in the scientific community at large—a community largely steeped in naturalism. It is necessary, though, to stick with the facts and see where the evidence leads, which is precisely what Behe is attempting to do. In a chapter entitled "Intelligent Design," he speaks of the inference of design in the world

---

12   John Lennox, "A Matter of Gravity - God, the Universe and Stephen Hawking" (2013), http://www.youtube.com/watch?v=1Xy4gMVlUCE; accessed March, 2014.

around us. Addressing the issue of whether it is truly reasonable to infer that design is evident in biological systems, he argues, "The greater the specificity of the interacting components required to produce the function, the greater is our confidence in the conclusion of design." Then, illustrating his point, says,

> This can be seen clearly in examples from diverse systems. Suppose that you and your spouse are hosting another couple one Sunday afternoon for a game of Scrabble. When the game ends, you leave the room for a break. You come back to find the Scrabble letters lying in the box, some face up and some face down. You think nothing of it until you read that the letters facing up read, "TAKE US OUT TO DINNER CHEAPSKATES." In this instance you immediately infer design, not even bothering to consider that the wind or an earthquake or your pet cat might have fortuitously turned over the right letters. You infer design because a number of separate components (the letters) are ordered to accomplish a purpose (the message) that none of the components could do by itself. Furthermore, the message is highly specific; changing several of the letters would make it unreadable. For the same reason, there is no gradual route to the message: one letter does not give you part of the message, a few more letters does not give a little more of the message, and so on.[13]

---

[13]   Michael Behe, *Darwin's Black Box: The Biochemical Challenge to Evolution* (New York: Simon and Schuster, 1996, 1998), 194.

The point Behe reiterates throughout the book is that what is observed today could not have developed in a gradual, naturalistic manner. The human eye, for example, is a complete unit of many separate parts working together. If one part is taken away, the eye no longer works. Therefore, it would be impossible for this system to develop in a gradual, completely naturalistic manner. There must be a Creator and Designer behind it all. The many complex biological systems and all of the intricate parts that work together in order to accomplish a specific purpose are powerful evidence of this.[14]

Going back to Paul's letter, this is one of the ideas he is bringing out so clearly. As quoted earlier, he says, "What may be known about God is plain to them, because God has made it plain to them. For since the creation of the world God's invisible qualities—his eternal power and divine nature—have been clearly seen, being understood from what has been made, so that people are without excuse" (Romans 1:19–20 NIV). In other words, people have an inherent knowledge of God as being the source of the world around them.

The boldness of Paul's statement is doubtless grating to many modern ears. Some have claimed that this idea is simply a "god-of-the-gaps" theory that in no way proves the existence of God. But this criticism confuses mechanism with agency, as again Lennox helps us to understand. It is like saying Henry Ford is a designer of the gaps simply because the mechanism he has designed functions on its own. Internal combustion is the mechanism that makes the car

---

[14] It takes great mental gymnastics to deny a designer and postulate how complex systems could have possibly developed on their own, especially as we discover more and more astonishing details through science.

work, but Ford is the explanation of its existence in the first place.[15] Beyond this, some may still argue that if God does exist, then He ought to be able to be perceived physically. This demand makes an unwarranted assumption about the nature of God. Later, the issue of whether God has revealed Himself physically will be discussed, but for now it must be remembered that God is not a created, physical entity and has no obligation to reveal Himself physically. Rather, Paul's idea is that the incredible design of everything in the universe shows us a great deal about God, which ought to be sufficient for what we generally need to know about His existence.

What Life Shows

So what can be learned of this Creator by looking at the world? One thing that makes an impression is the vast enormity of the universe. I have always enjoyed looking at the stars, but they became an even greater source of wonder when I as a grade-schooler learned that the nearest star (other than the sun) is about four light years away. This means that one would have to travel at the speed of light, which is 186,000 miles per second, for four years to make it to the nearest star. This is mind-boggling when one considers that there are billions of stars in our own galaxy. But even more astonishing is to see pictures taken by the Hubble Space Telescope revealing many distant galaxies, which themselves appear like tiny stars from so far away, and each galaxy consists of billions of stars that are all light years away from each other!

---

[15] John Lennox, "Not the God of the Gaps, But the Whole Show" (2012), http://www.christianpost.com/news/the-god-particle-not-the-god-of-the-gaps-but-the-whole-show-80307/; accessed March, 2014.

In contemplating the cosmos, the ancient psalmist states, "When I consider Your heavens, the work of Your fingers, The moon and the stars, which You have ordained, What is man that You are mindful of him, And the son of man that You visit him?" (Psalm 8:3–4 NKJV). Looking at the size of the heavens caused this man to sense just how small he truly was and to ask, "Why would the God who created all of this take notice of humans?" He was truly in awe of the greatness of the universe, and this is considering he knew far less than we do about space. How much more should we be in awe of the incredible vastness of creation?

Another aspect of life is its complexity. There are countless examples of this, but consider just a couple. Mark Looy writes,

> The adult brain—weighing only about three pounds and averaging about 1400 cubic centimeters—contains about ten billion (10^{10}) neurons. The neuron (or nerve cell) is the basic unit of the brain. Each contains branching fibers, called dendrites, and each neuron is in dendritic contact with as many as 10,000 other neurons. Amazingly, the total number of neuron interconnections (also called "bits") is approximately 1000 trillion (10^{15}), and if the dendritic connections were laid end to end, they would circle the earth more than four times…
>
> In his iconoclastic volume, *Evolution: A Theory in Crisis*, evolutionist Michael Denton has offered the following descriptive observation and analogy regarding the brain's 10^{15} connections:
>
> Numbers in the order of 10^{15} are of course completely beyond comprehension. Imagine an area about half the size of the USA (one million

square miles) covered in a forest of trees containing ten thousand trees per square mile. If each tree contained ten thousand leaves, the total number of leaves in the forest would be 10^{15}, equivalent to the number of connections in the human brain.[16]

The brain is like an unfathomably complex computer, but perhaps even more astonishing are discoveries about DNA. Just a pinhead amount contains enough information to fill a pile of books that would reach five hundred times further than the moon.[17] Life's complexity is utterly astounding.

Again, the psalmist's writing offers a similar insight: "I will praise You, for I am fearfully and wonderfully made" (Psalm 139:14). He certainly did not have our scientific understanding, but he was nevertheless amazed at the incredible design of the human body. We too cannot help but be amazed by the complexity of everything seen in creation. It is so complex that even in an age of such great technological advances, we are overwhelmed by the ingenuity of its design.

Life is also characterized by beauty. Whether it be the snow-covered mountains, a glorious sunset, a flowering garden, or a stirring piece of music, people are deeply moved by the beauty they experience each and every day, and these things are just the tip of the iceberg. There are countless other examples of how our world is filled with incredible beauty.

---

[16] Mark Looy, "I Think, Therefore There is a Supreme Thinker" (available at http://www.icr.org/article/335/; accessed February, 2014).
[17] Werner Gitt, "Dazzling Design in Miniature", http://creation.com/dazzling-design-in-miniature-dna-information-storage-creation-magazine.

I could certainly go on far longer describing the different characteristics of life, but my ultimate point is that life evokes a common response in people, a response of wonder, amazement, joy, and gratitude (such as what I experienced at the birth of my son). Now, whether we realize it or not, this response is actually what might be called worship. Some may not call it that because it sounds too religious, but that is, in essence, what it is. Even the atheist Richard Dawkins said as much.

> When I lie on my back and look up at the Milky Way on a clear night and see the vast distances of space and reflect that these are also vast differences of time as well, when I look at the Grand Canyon and see the strata going down, down, down, through periods of time which the human mind can't comprehend, I'm overwhelmingly filled with a sense of, almost worship... it's a feeling of sort of an abstract gratitude that I am alive to appreciate these wonders, when I look down a microscope it's the same feeling, I am grateful to be alive to appreciate these wonders.[18]

Worship is the natural response all humans have when they experience the many wonderful facets of life. This is seen in the way people act toward great musicians, artists, or athletes. Their talents create a sense of awe and pleasure in others, leading to great admiration or even adoration. Hence, people clap and cheer loudly for them at a performance or event. Often, many are seen mobbing

---

18   Richard Dawkins, "Atheism is the New Fundamentalism" (debate sponsored by Intelligence Squared), 2009.

together just to get a glimpse of a particular person or stand in a very long line just to attain an autograph. People at times even become obsessed with these icons. All of this is encapsulated in the term *worship*.

God Is Most Important

There is a great problem here, though. While life evokes a response of worship within each and every person—and rightly so—many people, without realizing it, are aiming their worship in the wrong place. Humans, unfortunately, have a tendency to worship either other people, as was already pointed out, or a particular thing about life. Some find great satisfaction in nature itself, some enjoy music, some are infatuated with attaining financial success, and so on, but the point is that everyone is obsessed with some person or thing that they truly find pleasure in or worship. What matters most to us is ultimately what we are worshipping.

The problem is that many are forgetting what is most important and what should be the true object of worship—the source from which everything we love and enjoy comes. It is akin to enjoying all the kind benefits my wife supplies for me but never bothering to acknowledge or thank her. This is very thing many people do every day in relation to God. He has provided a world with so much to be inspired by and enjoy, but instead of worshipping Him, many are worshipping what He has given them.

In reality, God deserves to be worshipped above all things because He is the source of all things. Therefore, when someone performs music beautifully, we should not idolize that individual but ought to be grateful to God for the musical talent He bestowed upon that person, grateful for the music itself, which He created, grateful for the ears to hear, which He designed, and grateful for the heart that can be touched with emotion, which He imparted to each of us. This applies not only to our enjoyment of music but also to all that we enjoy. So in looking at the miracle of life, we are directed toward the Giver of Life and see that He deserves our worship. If life matters, then God, the source of it, matters most and should be treated as such.

CHAPTER 4

PICTURE PERFECT

It seemed to be a typical day as Americans awoke and went about their business that September morning. Little did they know the world-changing events that were about to take place. Most people remember exactly where they were when given the earth-shattering news about the terrorist attacks, and many of us watched with horror and grief as we witnessed the collapse of the World Trade Center, serious damage inflicted on the Pentagon, and a plane taken down and prevented from doing further damage by some heroic passengers. What I keenly remember in the following days and weeks, though, was the sense of unity Americans had and the desire to bring to justice the perpetrators of these horrific actions. These deep-hearted sentiments reveal another aspect of life that matters to each of us: morality, the sense of what is right and wrong.

Many people are content to think of God as merely some distant designer or life-giving force that brought everything into existence, but the moral consciousness possessed by humans indicates something more. Instilled within us is a notion of the importance of doing what is right and standing against what is wrong. Admittedly, ethics has become a murky issue in a culture that avoids absolutes, yet one still cannot escape how deeply the human spirit resonates with a sense of morality. An experience of Ravi Zacharias speaks to this. He recounts,

> At a recent meeting I was addressing in Hong Kong, a businessman stood up and proposed that all values were just contrived and had no bearing on ultimate reality. After I answered his question, I invited him to come and have a personal talk on the subject. He took me up on the offer, and with a crowd of people straining their necks to listen in on the conversation, I said to him that by inference one could assume that he denied that any act was intrinsically evil.
>
> "That is a correct inference," he said.
>
> Hardly believing the hole he had dug for himself, I asked him the obvious. "Suppose I were to take a newborn baby, bring it to this platform, and proceed with a sharp sword to mutilate that child. Are you saying to me that there is nothing actually wrong or evil in that deed?"
>
> To the stunned expressions of those listening in, he shrugged and shifted and then said, "I may not like it, but I cannot call it morally wrong."
>
> There was only one thing left to say. "How incongruous it is, even by your own philosophy, that while denying the fact of evil you are unable to completely shake off the feeling… for even you, sir, said you would not like it. An understatement I hope."[19]

---

[19] Ravi Zacharias, *Deliver Us from Evil* (Dallas, TX: Word Publishing), 181–82.

This account is a powerful illustration of two things. The first is how morally confused some people have become in a postmodern context, even denying that mutilating a child is truly wrong. The second, a great relief, is that in spite of moral denial, people cannot help reacting strongly against those things that they feel and, deep down know, to be wrong. Morality may be a clouded and heavily debated topic in our society, but it is clearly something that is important and occupies a great deal of human attention.

The Standard of Morality

At the beginning of his book *Mere Christianity*, C. S. Lewis discusses the fascinating tendency for humans to argue and what this reveals. Whether it be children arguing over someone cutting ahead in line or adults arguing about a deep issue, such as abortion, there is one thing all of these arguments have in common: we are trying to prove that we are right and "the other man is in the wrong."[20] Lewis says,

> Now what interests me about all these remarks is that the man who makes them is not merely saying that the other man's behaviour does not happen to please him. He is appealing to some kind of standard of behaviour which he expects the other man to know about.[21]

Without even realizing it, people are engaging in a particular activity all the time: they are holding each other accountable to a

---

[20] Lewis, *Mere Christianity*, 4.
[21] Ibid., 3.

certain standard or moral law. They expect others to be fair, to not steal, to not kill innocent people, and whenever someone breaks this standard, that person is treated with, at the very least, disapproval.

This standard becomes a basis for evaluating others. If someone seems to live up to this standard, then people look up to and may even praise that person. Hence, we see how many people admired and spoke highly of Mother Theresa because she epitomized many people's idea of a moral person. She not only refrained from wrongdoing, such as stealing, lying, hatred, etc., but she also gave so much to help those in need, exhibiting compassion, love, and generosity toward others. A life such as this stirs up a sense of admiration and respect because it exudes so many of the qualities considered to be morally good.

On the other hand, people seem to have the opposite reaction toward those who do not live up to that standard very well. Generally those who are liars, cheaters, hateful, thieves, and so on are regarded in a negative way. People who grossly violate this standard, such as Hitler or Stalin, are looked at as evil, worthy of nothing but great disdain. The apparent reason for this judgment is because of the sense that people ought to live according to the moral standard to which all are accountable. It is, therefore, a universal moral law.[22]

This idea greatly bothers certain people who are more comfortable with a relativistic approach to such matters, but it must be noted that if one does not believe in a universal standard, then there is no basis for stating that people, such as Hitler and the Nazis, are doing something wrong. And there are no grounds for asserting that they should be held accountable regardless of whether they agree with the one making the judgment. If the answer to this objection

---

[22] This is not to say that all people believe it is a universal law but that in practice a standard is being applied universally.

is that society determines the moral standard, one is still left with the issue that our society is judging another society. In other words, we are still appealing to a standard that is even above society itself, which is the basis for saying the Nazi society is guilty.

Living up to the Standard

If there is truly a universal standard by which others are evaluated, which in practice is how humanity operates, then it behooves us to ask how we are living up to this standard. The typical person would probably answer that, overall, he is a good person. As a matter of fact, the common consensus today is that mankind, on the whole, is good. However, if one takes an honest assessment of the history and even the present-day condition of humanity, good does not seem an apt description, to say the least.

In reality, mankind has not had a history of long periods of peace with occasional spells of war but rather just the opposite. Humans are always fighting and struggling to have peace, even for a brief moment. While it is claimed that humanity has made great progress in the last few centuries, this certainly does not pertain to morality. Wars have certainly not subsided; technology has only made them more devastating! And one must not forget all that it takes to curb crime and maintain peace within a country—laws, police, courts, jails, surveillance cameras, locks, security systems, etc. If mankind is ultimately good, then the need for all of these safety measures is quite puzzling.

Some might say that it is the badness of a select few that spoils everything for the rest of us, but the truth is that we all have the capacity as well as the tendency to do that which leads to turmoil and dysfunction. It ought to be an indicator of our condition that when people get married (two people who are supposedly good and who supposedly love each other very much), they do not find it "easy" to live in harmony. In fact many marriages end in divorce, and many people today are avoiding marriage altogether. The truth is that people struggle to do what they know to be good, even when they have every reason to be good. The glib and all-too-common answer to all of this is to say, "Well, nobody's perfect," as if that somehow excuses the fact that one has failed to do what is right. In reality, human experience demonstrates that *no one* is living up to the universal moral standard, even those who are considered to be good people.

Ironically, when individuals are pinned up against the wall and are clearly shown just how bad they are, they are quick to respond by saying it is not really their fault. They try to blame their weaknesses on family upbringing, or they might claim the conditions of society set them up for failure. What this overlooks is that family and society are made up of people, which brings us back to the initial point: people are failing to live up to the universal moral standard; they are not ultimately good. Furthermore, even if a person's family was not a good one, there is no viable reason for blaming them for one's behavior. A person can choose to respond to others however he wishes. Thus, if one responds to an imperfect father with hatred, instead of loving him and trying to understand him, that person has failed just as much as his parent in doing what is right.

The fact is, we are all guilty of breaking the moral law, though we may try with all of our might to dismiss or excuse it. Once again, following the line of Paul's argument, he claims, "No one is righteous—not even one" (Romans 3:10 NLT). In this context, he is addressing those who have been brought up in Judaism and are religious. Even they, says Paul, are not truly righteous. They may judge others based on a moral standard, but when applied to themselves, they fall short as well. Each and every one of us has failed to keep moral perfection.

Behind the Moral Law

Many people try to console themselves with the thought even though they have broken the universal standard (or moral law), they have followed it more times than not. They believe that all of the good things they do in keeping with the moral law must account for some credit that will offset their failures. While this may seem valid on the surface, their logic fails to account for the reality of how a law operates.

When it comes to accountability to a law, there are really only two types of people: those who are guilty and those who are not. This is true regardless of how many times a person has kept the law, for the moment he breaks it, he immediately becomes guilty. When someone is pulled over for speeding, for example, the police officer has seen that the law of the speed limit has been broken, and the person, therefore, is considered guilty and must pay the fee owed for breaking the law. Now that person may protest and argue that he should not get a ticket because he follows the speed limit 99 percent of the time, but all of his good driving will earn him nothing because it doesn't negate the fact that he has broken the law and is guilty.

Likewise, it would be appalling if a man who was shown to be a murderer asked the court not to sentence him because most of the time he had been good and not killed anyone. That may be true, but the law holds him accountable for murdering a person regardless of how good he has been to everyone else. This is the nature and purpose of any law. It sets a standard for how people ought to behave and brings guilt and judgment upon them the moment they do not obey the law.[23] Therefore, the fact that we do not always keep the universal moral law makes us guilty, and there is no way around it.

Getting back to the initial discussion, this moral law is a reminder, once again, of the knowledge people have beyond the physical realm. They know that they should behave a certain way and feel guilty if they do not, and they know this just as surely as they know that two plus two is four. This innate knowledge points toward the reality of a moral lawgiver (the basis for this standard to which all are accountable), and we are brought back once again to the source of all life and the source of this moral law: God.

To think of God as the source of life is one thing, but to think of Him as the source of the moral law is something entirely different and even downright unsettling if one really ponders this thought. But no matter how much one may be tempted to fight against this idea, it is vital to honestly consider the facts.

It was pointed out earlier how people evaluate others, or judge them, according to the moral law. This is why people become angry with or look down on those who do something they know to be wrong, such as stealing or lying, but there is an implication Paul draws from this.

> You may think you can condemn such people, but you are just as bad, and you have no excuse! When you say they are wicked and should be punished, you are condemning yourself, for you who judge others do these very same things. And we know that God, in his justice, will punish anyone who

---

[23] It is interesting to note how many people are appalled upon finding out that someone who seemed to be nice and respectable actually committed a heinous crime. Niceness must never be equated with inherent goodness.

does such things. Since you judge others for doing
these things, why do you think you can avoid God's
judgment when you do the same things? (Romans
2:1–3 NLT)

In other words, if one knows enough about morality to judge
other people as being wrong in what they do, how will the God who
gave the moral law in the first place deal with each of *us*, who are
also breakers of His law? One can only assume that God will hold
each and every person accountable. He has established a law that all
are aware of and hold each other accountable to, and He has given
humans a clear sense of guilt when that law is broken. The moral
law indicates human accountability before a morally perfect God.

What would it be like to meet this perfect being? It is possible,
based on the evidence observed so far, to infer that it would be
terrifying. Many people think of the perfection or holiness of God as
a wonderful thing, but if one fully considers what it would feel like
to have all of one's guilt fully exposed in the presence of perfection,
it is obvious that it would be far from wonderful. The Bible indicates
that what a person would naturally feel in the presence of the perfect
one is an overwhelming sense of guilt, shame, and fear.[24] The reason
so many of us miss this is because we, as humans, are so distant from
the concept of perfection that we ignore and may even ridicule the
idea that God is to be feared.

Think for a moment, though, of what it is like to have our
guilt exposed. One story that reminds me of this concept is when
my oldest son was two and my oldest daughter was one. They were
supposed to be upstairs sleeping in their room, but I kept hearing

---

[24] This was the prophet Isaiah's reaction when he had a vision of being
in the presence of God in Isaiah 6:1–5.

the pitter-patter of tiny little feet racing across the floor. After a little while, I went upstairs to see what was going on. As I opened the door, I saw a very interesting sight. My son was in my daughter's playpen, along with my daughter, and every toy they owned was piled in with them. Both of them had a look of dread on their faces as they looked up at me. Why? Because they knew judgment day had come and they were guilty.

Now even though this is a lighthearted example, I hope no one will disregard the seriousness of what this incident illustrates. When I was not with them, my children were enjoying themselves, even though they were doing something wrong, but the moment they were in the presence of the one who would hold them accountable for their actions, they were filled with guilt and fear. The fact is, they were guilty even before they saw me, but they ignored this fact until it was too late. Unfortunately, this is exactly what many are doing in relation to God, and though right now they may be enjoying themselves and ignoring the guilt within, there is the awful thought that one day they will be exposed and held accountable for their actions. As one writer in the Bible indicates, "It is a fearful thing to fall into the hands of the living God" (Hebrews 10:31 NKJV).

Considering the Consequences

It is easy for people in our increasingly secular culture to glibly dismiss all of this as religious extremism. However, to fully grasp the seriousness of the situation, one must get beyond the idea that people merely make mistakes at times. Building on what has been discussed to this point, moral violations have great significance, for everything a person does wrong is ultimately in relation to God. When people steal from others or show hatred, they are not only wronging other people but ultimately are wronging the one who is the source of every person's life. It is somewhat akin to how my friend recently had her car vandalized. Not only was the car affected (directly), but my friend who owns the car was affected (indirectly) as well. God, the Creator and owner of all things, is constantly incurring the damage of our law-breaking lives by the way we treat the people and things He has created. When we hurt His creations, we are acting against Him, whether we mean to or not. On top of this, we also directly affect Him by failing to thank, love, and honor Him even though He is the one who gave us everything we have, including our very lives. Then, to top it off, we become angry at the thought of God judging, as if He has no right or grounds to do so.

What would people think of a child who continually broke his parents' rules without remorse, enjoyed all of the things his parents had given him (such as food, clothing, shelter, material possessions, enjoyable experiences, etc.), but never showed appreciation or love for his parents and became angry and resentful when they showed disapproval over his behavior? Likely the response would be that this child was being an ungrateful brat who deserved some negative consequences. This sheds some light on how humans are behaving in relation to God. The difference, however, is that the child is rebelling against parents who, though they may be wonderful parents, are also imperfect and are created entities. God, in contrast, is perfect and is the source of everything. If treating humans wrongly merits repercussions, then treating God wrongly is of even greater consequence. This leads to yet another topic of importance.

CHAPTER 5

APPOINTMENT WITH DEATH

One evening, several years ago, I was lying in my bed waiting for my wife to come upstairs. We were living at my in-laws' house at the time, looking to buy a house of our own. It had been an eventful Sunday. I had spent the day with my wife and her family going to church and eating lunch together, and in the evening, all of us went to a church in Vermont to give a family concert. It was a great joy to perform with the family as we sang about God and our love for Him. It was one of many good days I have had worshipping God and spending time with family, and I remember feeling so content about everything we had done that day as I was lying in my bed.

It seemed to be taking a while for my wife to come to bed. Finally, I heard her running up the stairs, which was a relief, but my heart immediately sank as she burst open the door and with a look of sheer horror and panic, ran to me and said the words I least expected to hear and will never forget: "My brother is dead!" I immediately put my arms around her and tried to comfort her. We then went downstairs, and I spent the next few hours helplessly trying to be of some comfort to my wife's parents. They were in severe agony over the sudden death of their own son, who we had just been with about an hour earlier.

Words cannot describe the intense emotional pain I witnessed that night. One particular emotion that stood out for me was a sense of dread. It was dreadful to consider the fact that my brother-in-law Scott had died in a car accident just hundreds of feet away from the driveway of my in-laws' home. He was a twenty-one-year-old young man who was engaged to be married to a woman he had met at college. He had been working hard at the time to save up money for the marriage and honeymoon, working two jobs with long hours, even working overnight. It was apparently due to the lack of sleep that he had become overly tired as he was driving, fell asleep at the wheel, and hit an oncoming vehicle on the other side of the road.

The sense of dread I felt that evening is a grim reminder of the reality of another important matter, one that most would rather not think or talk about: death. However, it was not just the issue of death that gripped my heart but the manner in which death had occurred. God could have kept my brother-in-law safe for a few hundred more feet, couldn't He? Some would say that He *should* have kept him safe, especially considering he was considered a morally upright young man with a fiancée and a good plan for his life. Instead, God allowed Scott to be taken at that instant, a person who we least expected to die at a moment we least expected him to be taken. Why would God allow this?

Situations like this reveal that God is not always the way humans expect or want Him to be. One reason some do not believe in God is because they expect God to act benevolently. However, many times God does things that are, from a human perspective, harsh and even dreadful. Several years ago, the world saw a tsunami take the lives of one hundred and fifty thousand people at once. Tragedies such as this are evidence that God permits circumstances that a merely benevolent creator would never allow.

A Purpose for Death

Death itself is an extremely perplexing issue to many people today. We live in a society whose main ideals are tolerance and kindness, and death seems so opposed to our sense of goodness. It is easy for people in this culture to conclude, therefore, that death is a horrible thing, and that is all there is to it. This causes great difficultly as one thinks of death in relation to God because it is hard to see how a good God would allow something as horrible as death. But one must be careful in jumping to the conclusion that death is exclusively bad, especially in light of what has been shown up to this point. It is true that death for no reason would not be a good thing, but could it be that God has a reason for death that many people are overlooking? I believe this to be the case.

The only way to understand how death can be a good thing is to change our frame of reference. Humans tend to think about death from a limited perspective that impedes their ability to see the bigger picture. It is, of course, very tragic to experience the death of a loved one. On another level, however, it is still possible for death to exist for a good reason. It is interesting to note, for example, how people feel about the death of a bad guy in a movie. Why are they satisfied to see someone die in this instance? It is because it is a good thing that evil has been eradicated, and a sense of justice has been met. Or for a real-life example, take the death of cruel dictators and terrorists. People believed, and rightfully so, that it is a good thing that all of the turmoil and suffering they were causing had come to an end. Death, though tragic in itself, can serve a good purpose.

With this in mind, let us return to the concepts outlined in the previous chapters. God is the source of life and the giver of all that is good, and God is also perfect and completely good in and of Himself. As He looks at mankind, what does He see? He sees people who are not grateful toward Him and who hardly acknowledge Him, if at all. In fact, He sees people who are filled with propensities like greed, bitterness, lust, hatred, deceit, and all of the things that have plagued humanity throughout history. So what is God to do?

Well, if God is truly good and just, He ought to do something about it. And this is where death comes into play. It could be seen as God's means of dealing with evil, of bringing the world to justice. All people are under a death penalty, so to speak.

God's Prerogative

It is natural to recoil from the proposition of God handling things in this manner. But I believe one reason people have a hard time with this is because humans are not truly good, and therefore they struggle to see their true condition in relation to a morally perfect being. They fail to understand God's prerogative, in perhaps a similar way to how a criminal may not agree with how a judge and jury handles his case (after all, he had good reasons for committing his crime, or his sentence does not seem fair in his eyes, etc.). Consider Saddam Hussein's reaction during his trial. According to a news report, in reaction to his death sentence, he cursed at the court and shouted, "You don't decide anything, you are servants of the occupiers and lackeys! You are puppets!"[25]

It is easy for humans to have a similar self-justified reaction in relation to God. This is where one must go back to the premise that all people are guilty of breaking the moral standard that God

[25]   Ellen Knickmeyer, "Hussein Sentenced To Death By Hanging" (available at http://www.washingtonpost.com/wp-dyn/content/article/2006/11/05/AR2006110500135_2.html; accessed February 2014).

has set in place. It doesn't matter how one compares to others; what matters is how one compares to God's perfection. To God, all of us may evoke the reaction that a (fill-in-the-blank with a behavior that deeply offends and angers you) might evoke in us. We may stand in moral judgment over others at times for some reason, but God stands in moral judgment over all of us for many reasons.

In the language of the courtroom, all people stand guilty before the Judge of the universe, and this Judge has chosen to sentence each and every person to death. Now one may protest and say that the Judge is too harsh (again the Hussein reflex arising), but let us remember two things. The first is that if God is truly a good Judge, he will not let anyone off the hook for breaking the law, no matter what excuse he or she may try to give. The second is that if this Judge is the source of life, and if we do not abide by His law, then He has every right to cut us off from Himself. But then, if we are cut off from our source of life, what is the result? Death! So death is not extreme; it is simply the natural correlation, the rightful sentence placed upon humans because of their guilt.

This (as you might have guessed by now) is Paul's logic as well in his letter to the Roman Christians. He describes death in direct connection with the judgment of God. Throughout chapter 5 of the letter, he continually shows the tie between sin (our unrighteousness, which makes us guilty before God) and death. Then, in the next chapter he makes a summary statement that "the wages of sin is death" (Romans 6:23a ESV). There is a second part to this statement that I will get to later, but at this point I want to highlight this particular concept. Paul is stating that our moral failure (sin) has a payment attached to it, and this payment is death.

I realize that this idea is very difficult for people in our culture to accept (including myself at times). But Paul must not be accused of introducing a novel teaching on the subject of death. He was following the teaching of Jesus, who gave an interesting response when asked about tragedy.

> About this time Jesus was informed that Pilate had murdered some people from Galilee as they were offering sacrifices at the Temple. "Do you think those Galileans were worse sinners than all the other people from Galilee?" Jesus asked. "Is that why they suffered? Not at all! And you will perish, too, unless you repent of your sins and turn to God. And what about the eighteen people who died when the tower in Siloam fell on them? Were they the worst sinners in Jerusalem? No, and I tell you again that unless you repent, you will perish, too." (Luke 13:1–5 NLT)

Most people in our society would probably think that if Jesus were approached about the issue of why bad things happen to people, He would offer some comforting, reassuring response. But when Jesus was approached about this very issue, He shockingly said that the people who died in these situations did not receive something undeserved and that anyone who does not repent (turn his life around) will face the same consequence. Not exactly a very kind and comforting answer, but Jesus was not trying to be diplomatic. He was expressing what He knew to be true, and what good would it have been if He had said something nicer if it was falsely assuring? But people in our world would often rather be consoled with theory than confronted with fact.

According to Jesus, death is something all people deserve. One can choose to disagree with this statement, but one cannot get around the fact that this was Jesus' perspective and teaching. So

Paul, as a follower of Christ, is echoing what Jesus said, and I am merely echoing both of them on this issue.

A New Perspective

I realize the subject of this chapter is troubling, and I promise there is something hopeful to come in the following chapters. But before moving on, I want to close with some important thoughts on this matter.

The first is that, no matter how much one may be averse to this topic, death is an unavoidable fact of life, one that we can either avoid or from which we can learn. Perhaps a change of perspective is in order. Instead of seeing humanity as the focal point of the universe and questioning God for allowing human death, one might consider the matter from a God-centered perspective. We are here because God has put us here; we are dependent on Him. He is in a different place of order than we are: He is Creator, and we are created. For that reason, God has the right to place Himself above all things and to deal with humanity as He deems fit. It is His prerogative to do so, though that may be hard for humans to accept.[26]

Second, the situation described thus far insinuates no obligation on the part of God to treat humans benevolently. There is no reason necessitated by the evidence observed to this point for why anyone should take for granted that this God should help us out of this predicament. I should remind the reader, too, that the common view of God in our culture, a god whose goal is solely human happiness (or ought to be), is in complete incongruity with the reality of death (and many other aspects of this world). Some have

---

[26] This includes both the fact of death and the timing of death.

chosen simply not to believe in a God who would make a world such as this, but distaste for implications is no reasonable grounds for rejecting God's existence. Others think that God must not be in control of everything, but this is hard to believe in light of the power necessary to bring the universe into existence in the first place. To accept that God can create the world but not control it seems inconsistent. While these alternative options may be more palatable to our modern sensitivities, I do not think they are logically sustainable, and neither are they safe. No matter how much one may be inclined to disregard all of this, death is a reality that each of us must face, and I believe it is wise to consider its significance.

CHAPTER 6

LOVE... TRUE LOVE

In the movie *The Princess Bride*, Miracle Max is asked to bring a "mostly dead" man named Wesley back to life for the sake of true love. In response, he says, "Sonny, true love is the greatest thing in the world, except for a nice MLT—mutton, lettuce and tomato sandwich." Though satirical in nature, the whole story revolves around this theme of true love. But as silly as this movie is, true love certainly is a very important aspect of life. This is evident in how much people write, talk, and sing about it. Of all that matters to us as humans, love stands in a high place, perhaps the highest place of all. It is the supreme virtue and the culmination of what is regarded as truly good. Perhaps this is why people are so obsessed with it. As much as they may enjoy possessions, food, or entertainment, all of these things pale in comparison to the value of love. While I cannot vouch for Miracle Max's preference for mutton, lettuce, and tomato sandwiches, I would agree that true love is of utmost importance to human experience.

The Great Dilemma

Now, in thinking about love in relation to God, it seems logical to infer that if love is so important and foundational to the human understanding of goodness, then a perfectly good God would also be a God of love. While it may be reasonable to make this assumption, many people immediately conclude that God indiscriminately loves everyone, and this becomes the exclusive framework for how they view God. They then conclude that they do not have to worry about His judgment because a loving God would not inflict judgment. But one must be very cautious about jumping to this conclusion, for there are two serious problems that must considered. The first problem is that, as already seen, God is perfect and humanity's ways have violated His moral law. Therefore, even if God is loving by nature, He is under no obligation to act favorably toward humanity, for humans are essentially in opposition to Him in the way they have chosen to live. A very loving is man is under no obligation to seek the release of one who has stolen from him. He may choose to do so, but he does not have to, even if (or especially if) the thief derides him, saying, "Why are you pressing charges? I thought you were known for being such a loving and kind person. How could you!" This is almost some people's attitude toward God, as if His love binds him to let people off the hook.

Another problem is that even if, for some particular reason, God would choose to help people who have offended Him, there is a dilemma. God is a perfect judge, and all of us stand guilty before Him, deserving the sentence of death. Remember, a good judge cannot simply let people off the hook, for if he did so, he would not be just. A judge who always lets people violate the law would be considered evil, and the judge would in no way be justified by saying that he only did it because he loves criminals. Therefore, even if God loves people, this does not negate the necessity for justice.

This puts humanity in an extremely dire situation. People do not deserve God's favor; they are offensive to His perfect nature, and even if God does love them, they are still guilty before His law. The result is that mankind is estranged from God; there is a rift in the relationship between God and humans. Most people sense the alienation between God and mankind, and there seems to be an overall feeling of uncertainty and hopelessness that pervades our culture spiritually. But as I said at the outset, my purpose in writing is to give hope to those who are looking for answers, and I believe there is good reason to hope as we continue to examine the evidence.

The Written Word Revealed

The only way one could find hope at this point is if God were to reach out in some way. The problem we face is insurmountable from our end because there is nothing we can do to rectify the situation between us and God. Therefore, if there were any solution to all of this, God would have to be the one to help us, but there is no way of knowing that God will do anything about this situation unless He chooses to reveal Himself in some way.

It is here I would propose that God *has* taken the initiative to help us, and this is not based on mere wishful thinking. I think I have made it clear that I am only interested in the facts, and I would find no comfort in my situation before God unless there were good reason for it. But here is where I find a great cause for hope, not only for myself but for all who realize this. God is not only the source of life, the perfect lawgiver, and the great judge; He is also the one who has revealed Himself to mankind in an extraordinary way. My reason for believing this is found in the pages of Scripture, or what is often called the Bible. It is in these writings that we find great evidence that God has, in fact, revealed Himself and reached out to mankind. I do not expect all readers here to readily assent to my viewpoint. I am only trying to say that the Bible is worth everyone's consideration, regardless of what point of view he or she may have concerning religion.

If God wanted to reveal Himself, He would have to communicate to us in some way, just as all of us communicate in order to express who we are with one another. This, in essence, is what God has done through the written Word of Scripture. He has given people a means by which they can more fully understand who He is. Sadly, many today seem to think of the Bible as an outdated book, but when one begins to examine its content, it becomes clear that this book is unique. It contains profound insight into the greatest questions of life. As a matter of fact, the ideas that have already been explored in this book are found throughout the Scriptures, which is partly why I have already chosen to use the biblical book of Romans written by Paul in laying out my ideas. I wanted the reader to see that the Bible has much to say that is not only relevant but also necessary for people today.

Of course, many arguments have been taken up to discredit the reliability of the Bible, but I would say that those who have studied the Bible with an open mind and a sincere desire for truth have discovered that these criticisms are not as solid as they first appear. The Christian author Josh McDowell, for example, was once a great skeptic and sought to discredit his college friends' belief in the Bible. But after doing extensive study looking for evidence against the Bible, he says,

> I found evidence. Evidence in abundance. Evidence
> I would not have believed with my own eyes.

Finally I could come to only one conclusion: If I were to remain intellectually honest, I had to admit that the Old and New Testament documents were some of the most reliable writings in all of antiquity.[27]

McDowell has since gone on to write some very notable works in defense of the validity of the Scriptures. Lee Strobel, once an atheistic skeptic, is another example of someone who has become persuaded and written about evidence supporting the Bible's veracity.[28] It is not my intent at this point to give a detailed argument listing all of the evidence that supports the Bible's accuracy. I am only trying to show that the arguments often heard today should not be enough to dissuade someone from taking the Bible into consideration, and I would urge any reader who has serious questions concerning the Scriptures to study some of the works that have been written on this issue and most of all, read the Bible for him or herself.

I also realize that many people in our naturalistically minded culture tend to have a hard time accepting the miraculous nature of some of the events recorded in the Bible. This has been a stumbling block for certain people, but I would remind them that miracles, as recorded in the Bible, are simply God's intervention into His creation. While this may not be scientifically provable, there is nothing in science that disproves the possibility of God intervening in some way. In reality, this is a philosophical issue rather than a scientific one. I would also add that even naturalistic scientific

---

[27]   Josh McDowell, "My Story: Josh McDowell" (Available at http://www.cru.org/how-to-know-god/my-story-a-life-changed/my-story-josh-mcdowell.htm; accessed February, 2014).

[28]   For example, the book *The Case for Christ* outlines some of Strobel's significant findings on the subject.

theories, such as the existence and development of complex life by random processes, could be considered just as miraculous and improbable as anything found in Scripture.

Another problem people may have with the Bible is that the writers were unaware of many scientific facts that we know about today. This leads some to think that the biblical authors are in some way more ignorant than people today are about life, but this is an unfair conclusion. It may be true that they did not know much about technology (or at least our technology), but in looking at their writings, it could hardly be said that they were ignorant about philosophical and spiritual issues. Some of the most brilliant insights are found in ancient literature. Many authors of the past have stood the test of time and continue to be repeated for this very reason. Arbitrarily disregarding viewpoints from people before our time and holding to the notion that we know best today is what C. S. Lewis described as "chronological snobbery." Obviously, scientific study has added to human knowledge and understanding, but this does not discount the true insights of the past.

I want to make it clear here, though, that I am not merely saying the writers of Scripture were great thinkers. The Bible has a depth of wisdom that no amount of human intellect could possibly generate. These writers had the ability to see how all of the intricate aspects of life fit together, somewhat like a gigantic puzzle, and they had a straightforward manner of explaining the world around us that makes incredible sense. I find this aspect of the Bible to be quite fascinating, and it points to the premise of the Bible being God's revelation.

It could be likened to a murder mystery, such as one of Agatha Christie's novels. In many of these stories, there is a great detective who has the uncanny ability to take all of the little snippets of information and piece them together in order to find out what really happened, but the real reason these detectives are so incredible, in truth, is because they have information that the reader does not have. They are being fed information from the author of the story, who carefully formulated the entire situation and presented it in the first place. I believe the Bible writers had inside information, so to speak, from the Author of life, which is why their descriptions of all of the deep matters of life seem to line up perfectly with the reality of what is seen all around.

This was my main reason for pointing out the argument used by the Bible writer Paul, for in fact, everything I have been saying is an echo of what is written in the Scriptures, and the Scriptures are able to bring us to a fuller understanding about life. I mean to say here, for those who may be bothered that I am proposing personal knowledge of the truth, that there is nothing special about me or even those who wrote the Bible. What *is* special is the truth that has been revealed and the God who has revealed that truth.

The Human Word Revealed

In examining the message of the Bible, one of the most astonishing statements is found at the beginning of the book of John. John, who was one of the twelve disciples who traveled with Jesus, writes, "In the beginning was the Word, and the Word was with God, and the Word was God" (John 1:1 NKJV). Several verses later he states, "So the Word became human and made his home among us" (John 1:14 NLT). What is seen in these statements is a mind-boggling concept. The "Word" that was in the beginning with God and was God "became human." John goes on to explain that this man (the Word) is Jesus, and for the rest of the book, he gives an eyewitness account of his experiences as a follower of Jesus.

It is noteworthy that he refers to Jesus as the Word, for the Jews have always regarded the Word of God, which included the ancient writings of Moses and the prophets, as coming from God and carrying the authority of God Himself. So John is saying that, just as the Scriptures are from God and reveal God's person and nature, Jesus too is from God and is the physical manifestation of God's person and nature. Or as theologian A.W. Tozer puts it, Jesus is the "mind of God in expression."[29] This is taught in other places in the Bible, such as book of Hebrews, which describes Jesus as "the radiance of God's glory and the exact expression of His nature" (Hebrews 1:3a HCSB).

John, the follower of Jesus, also states, "He was in the beginning with God. All things were made through Him" (John 1:2–3a NKJV). This is a clear statement that Jesus, who was in the beginning, is the author of life. Paul brings this out as well in the book of Colossians where he writes the following:

> The Son [Jesus] is the image of the invisible God, the firstborn over all creation. For in him all things were created: things in heaven and on earth, visible and invisible, whether thrones or powers or rulers or authorities; all things have been created through him and for him. (Colossians 1:15–16 NIV)

And going back to John, he continues, "The Word gave life to everything that was created, and his life brought light to everyone. The light shines in the darkness, and the darkness can never extinguish it" (John 1:4–5 NLT). Jesus is described as the light,

---

[29] A. W. Tozer, *God Tells the Man Who Cares* (Camp Hill, PA: WingSpread Publishers, 1993; Kindle Edition), location 118.

which carries the idea of moral perfection, and He came to a world filled with darkness or wickedness and sin. John also clearly states in the book of 1 John, "In Him there is no sin" (1 John 3:5 NKJV). This is also stated by other eyewitness followers of Jesus, such as Peter, who says Jesus "did not commit sin, and no deceit was found in His mouth" (1 Peter 2:22 HCSB).

In continuing through the book of John, one sees that Jesus suffered a great deal. Most people are aware of the fact that Jesus was crucified, which was a form of torture carried out by the Roman Empire as a means of capital punishment. Jesus experienced incredible physical and emotional pain and even death.

So here is the connection between Jesus and all that that has been discussed up to this point: Jesus is the author of life, He is morally perfect, and He has experienced pain and death. Furthermore, Jesus' appearance on earth took place in order to bring about the most wonderful truth of all—that God Himself has chosen to experience what humans go through because of something so integral to humanity.

What God Demonstrated toward Us

It has already been shown that mankind is in a great dilemma in relation to God. So how could the perfectly holy Creator of the universe show love toward those who deserve His judgment? The answer is in Jesus.

Going back to Paul's letter to the Romans, one of the most thrilling statements in all of Scripture is given.

> When we were utterly helpless, Christ [Jesus] came
> at just the right time and died for us sinners. Now,

most people would not be willing to die for an upright person, though someone might perhaps be willing to die for a person who is especially good. But God showed his great love for us by sending Christ to die for us while we were still sinners. (Romans 5:6–8 NLT)

Paul has already made the case that mankind is guilty before God, but now he presents the purpose for the coming of Jesus, who he refers to as Christ or Messiah. He is saying that God sent His Son to demonstrate His great love! I hope the reader catches the sort of love that God demonstrates: love toward sinners. It is not love toward people who deserve His love but love toward people who do not deserve it, for they are, by their actions and attitudes, His enemies. They are sinners. Therefore, it is seen in what God has revealed about Himself that He does, in fact, love people, and it is a love that is incredible, costing Him the death of His Son!

But why did Christ have to die in order for God's love to be shown? This brings the discussion back to the problem that was presented at the outset. Even if God loves people, they deserve His judgment. So what did God do? He sent Jesus to face divine judgment on our behalf. The penalty of sin had to be paid, and Jesus paid it. As Paul states in the next verse, "And since we have been made right in God's sight by the blood of Christ, he will certainly save us from God's condemnation" (Romans 5:9 NLT).

Therefore, we can be saved from the judgment of God. Jesus' death is able to make us righteous before God because Jesus became the one who faced the judgment of God on our behalf. This is what the cross is all about. It is about God pouring out His wrath on His Son in order to satisfy His morally perfect justice. It was the only way by which humans could be saved. There is a story told from American history that elucidates these concepts.

> In a tribe of Indians, someone was stealing chickens. The chief declared that, if caught, the offender would receive 10 lashes. When the stealing continued, he raised it to 20 lashes. Still the chickens methodically disappeared. In anger the chief raised the sentence to 100 lashes—a sure sentence of death.
>
> The thief was finally caught. But the chief faced a terrible dilemma. The thief was his own mother!
>
> When the day of penalty came, the whole tribe gathered. Would the chief's love override his justice? The crowd gasped when he ordered his mother to be tied to the whipping post. The chief removed his shirt, revealing his powerful stature, and took the whip in hand. But instead of raising it to strike the first blow, he handed it to a strong, young brave at his side.
>
> Slowly the chief walked over to his mother and wrapped his massive arms around her in an engulfing embrace. Then he ordered the brave to give him the 100 lashes.[30]

God truly is the God of love. God's love is the culmination of His goodness. Love is not just something He has; it is a part of His very nature. The Bible says, "God is love" (1 John 4:8 NKJV). It is this love that has generated a plan in which mankind can be set

---

[30] Martin R. DeHaan II, "Why Did Christ Have to Die?" (Grand Rapids: RBC Ministries, 1991), 14–15.

free from God's judgment, forgiven, and restored to a close, loving relationship with God.

What one also reads in the Bible is that God is showing patience toward mankind, waiting for people to turn to Him. Unfortunately, many people mistake God's patience as a sign that He will not judge, but the disciple Peter states,

> Dear friends, don't let this one thing escape you: With the Lord one day is like a thousand years, and a thousand years like one day. The Lord does not delay His promise, as some understand delay, but is patient with you, not wanting any to perish but all to come to repentance. (2 Peter 3:8–9 HCSB)

God will judge human rebellion but is patiently waiting for people to repent or turn to Him.

Amazing Grace

In light of all of this, it is clear that the Bible, which reveals God's character and communication, gives a message of grace. But grace is a term that is difficult to fully understand. A very popular song over that past few hundred years and even today is "Amazing Grace." What I believe has caused this song to stand the test of time is that it speaks of something that touches the core of our being. Grace is love and kindness toward those who do not deserve it. As the songwriter puts it,

Amazing grace, how sweet the sound

That saved a wretch like me

I once was lost but now am found

Was blind but now I see

The writer of this song, John Newton, understood grace in a way that is often missed today.

John Newton was born in London in the year 1725. His father was a sea captain. His mother, a devout Christian woman who, realizing that an illness she had would take her life within a short time, taught her son to know the Bible at an early age.

When John was seven, his mother died and he became a cabin boy aboard a sailing ship. His experiences through the years on the sea were dangerous and exciting, even to being shanghaied. That is, he was forced to join the crew of a Man of War. Here he was cruelly treated, being flogged and abused. After this experience, he joined the crew of a slave ship and eventually became a captain. During all of this, John drifted far from his mother's God and the Bible. He later wrote, "I often saw the necessity of being a Christian as a means of escaping hell, but I loved sin and was unwilling to forsake it."

Each year saw him sinking lower into the pits of sin and soon he had gotten so low that even the ship's crew despised him as being no more than an animal. On one occasion, the drunk captain fell overboard but the men did not so much as make an effort to drop a boat over the side to rescue him. They simply took a whaling harpoon and threw it at him. It caught him in his hip and the crew hauled him aboard, much the same as they would a large fish. Because of this occurrence, John Newton limped the rest of his life, but as he would say, "Each limp is a constant reminder of God's grace to this wretched sinner."[31]

I believe the key to understanding grace is to see what Newton saw about himself. Notice that he refers to himself as a "wretch," and because he saw himself as an unworthy, helpless sinner, he was truly amazed that God had worked in his life and saved him. John Newton correctly saw God as being the greatest and most important, not himself. Sadly, many today think so highly of themselves that they fail to recognize that they are in need of God's grace. As author Tim Keller writes, "No one is so good that they don't need the grace of the gospel, nor so bad that they can't receive the grace of the gospel."[32] The Bible's message of grace is not about how we can somehow be good enough or worthy enough to get to God but about how God was willing to come to us, even though He did not have to. God is a God of love, and He has demonstrated love in the most incredible way. The question is: How will we respond?

---

[31] Alfred B. Smith, *Al Smith's Treasury of Hymn Histories* (Greenville, SC: Better Music Publication, Inc., 1981, 1982, 1985), 61–62.

[32] Tim Keller, *Galatians for You* (Purcellville, IN: The Good Book Co., 2013), 28.

CHAPTER 7

GETTING PERSONAL

I live in New England, where people are generally known to be more reserved. I have spoken with people from the South, who even felt that many New Englanders were downright cold. (What do you expect when living in climate like this, though?) I have found it humorous to have phone conversations that were over in ten words or less (mostly consisting of *my* words with a couple of yups on the other end). However, my time here over more than a decade has shown that people where I live may not open up quickly, but many of them are some of the most genuine, hard-working, loyal, and loving people one could ever meet. The only way to really understand people, though, no matter where one lives, is to develop a relationship with them, and this takes time and effort. But it is one of the most rewarding and meaningful aspects of life.

The importance of relationships is seen in many ways, such as in the friendships people share and enjoy throughout life. It would be difficult to overestimate the value of a good friendship, and one of the hardest things to do is say good-bye to a close friend. Families are also built upon a relationship of love, and the closeness people share within families as husbands, wives, parents, and children is invaluable. Of course, there are those who do not feel very close to their families, but even these individuals often wish they could have that kind of relationship within their family, which further reveals just how significant these relationships are to humans.

Relationships are so important that infants cannot survive without the caring interaction of another person. Children without good relationships often have great emotional turmoil, and teens and adults who struggle to find close relationships in some cases might even consider suicide as a better alternative than living a life of loneliness. There is no doubt that relationships are a vital aspect of human existence and experience.

The Source of Relationship

As with many of the topics that have been discussed already, it is often overlooked that the importance people attach to personal relationships has a direct connection with the way in which humans were designed. The reason humans are personal, meaning that they possess a self-consciousness and the ability and desire to know others who have a self-consciousness, is because they have been created as personal beings. And the reason they have been created as personal beings is because the Creator Himself is a personal Being.

God's love is not merely aimed at freeing people from judgment, though this certainly is very important, but it is also aimed at bringing them into a relationship with Him. When it comes to my children, for example, I love to do good things for them, but my love for them is not content with this. I want to know them, and I want

them to know me. This is the natural outgrowth of love. Love is the
seed from which the flowers of relationships grow.

Therefore, to say that God is love but to fail to recognize His
aim toward personal relationship is to miss the ultimate point. It is
like being content with the seed but never enjoying the flower or the
fruit. Tragically, there are many people who believe there may be a
God of love but completely dismiss the concept of having a personal
relationship with Him.

A Broken Relationship

There is a reason for humans' reluctance to come to God. Moral
guilt has alienated people from Him and has left a great gulf between
God and humanity. In other words, the skewed nature of humans
prevents them from being able to enjoy the presence of the one who
is perfectly pure. We are like children who are trying to hide from
their parents because they did something they know their parents
would not like.

It is always characteristic of humans to feel uncomfortable and
avoid being around people who they associate as being morally pure.
Many times I have been around people who felt free to talk and act
any way they pleased until they discovered that I am in the ministry.
Suddenly, they seem to act a bit embarrassed and self-conscious and
might even try say something to try to show that they are good
people. This is similar to the situation in a story told by R. C. Sproul.

> A few years ago one of the leading golfers on the
> professional tour was invited to play in a foursome
> with Gerald (then president of the United States),
> Jack Nicklaus, and Billy Graham. The golfer was

especially in awe of playing with Ford and Billy Graham.

After the round of golf was finished, one of the other pros came up to the golfer and asked, "Hey, what was it like playing with the president and Billy Graham?"

The pro unleashed a torrent of cursing, and in a disgusted manner said, "I don't need Billy Graham stuffing religion down my throat." With that he turned on his heel and stormed off, heading for the practice tee.

His friend followed the angry pro to the practice tee. The pro took out his driver and started to beat out balls in fury. His neck was crimson, and it looked as if steam was coming from his ears. His friend said nothing. He sat on a bench and watched. After a few minutes the anger of the pro was spent. He settled down. His friend said quietly, "Was Billy a little rough on you out there?"

The pro heaved an embarrassed sigh and said, "No, he didn't even mention religion. I just had a bad round."[33]

Sproul goes on to deduce that the man's discomfort had much to do with Billy Graham being identified with religion and the things of God. What is exposed by these instances is that people cannot escape the fact that they do not like being in the presence of moral purity because it exposes their own impurity or guilt. Now

---

[33] R.C. Sproul, *The Holiness of God* (Wheaton, IL: Tyndale House Publishers, 1985, 1998), 66–67.

if people feel uncomfortable around me, a very obviously imperfect person, how much more is this problem magnified in relation to God? There is not one person who would naturally feel comfortable in His presence and want to have a relationship with Him.

The Offer of a Restored Relationship

God, however, has provided a way in which people can be forgiven of their sins and stand before Him without guilt. Not only does this mean a person no longer has to fear punishment, but it also provides the basis on which one can have a personal relationship with Him. No longer does one have to run and hide from the presence of a morally perfect God because God is able and willing to make us clean. And without guilt, it is now possible to enjoy a close and loving relationship with Him. In the sight of God, anyone can be regarded as righteous and honorable as Billy Graham, regardless of what they have done.

The disciple John writes, "See what great love the Father has lavished on us, that we should be called children of God!" (1 John 3:1 NIV). Obviously, John was amazed at the love God has shown, but what specifically is so amazing about God's love? It is that it enables people to become "children of God." This is an incredible statement that speaks of a very special relationship. God, the one humans fear and avoid by nature, has shown His love through the sacrifice of His Son, and because of this, it is possible to become His child. Instead of relating to God as judge, it is possible to relate to Him as Father!

How This Relationship Comes About

All of this may sound well and good, but the critical question at this point is how does this take place? How can a person become a child of God (since the assumption according to the writers of Scripture is that people are not in God's family to begin with)? The Bible's answer to this is far different than what would be expected. Humans have an inherent tendency to think that they must earn God's favor in order to be accepted by Him. But this is the most wonderful and staggering thing about the biblical message: God does not expect people to try to earn His favor, for that is the opposite of grace. And the fact is, no one could ever do enough to earn God's favor anyway because, again, all humans are morally guilty, and trying to make up for it with good deeds does not change this.

So if good works are not the basis for finding forgiveness, then what is? Here is what Paul says in the beginning of the fifth chapter of Romans: "Therefore, since we have been declared righteous by faith, we have peace with God through our Lord Jesus Christ" (Romans 5:1 HCSB).

Paul has just finished a discussion looking at the example of Abraham, the greatly revered father of the Jews. Paul points out that, according to the Scriptures, Abraham believed God, and it was credited to him as righteousness (Genesis 15:6). Paul is using this as the foundation and example of how people can be made righteous, and he clearly states that people are considered righteous by faith. In other words, people must believe God, and when they trust Him, God will recognize that individual as being righteous, and this brings peace with God so a person is no longer at enmity with God. This, he says, is made possible through Christ, who provides access into God's grace because He took God's judgment of sin upon Himself (cf. Romans 5:8). As a result, a person with faith in Christ can stand confident in God's grace rather than his or her own goodness.

Faith, therefore, is the key that opens the door to God's household. God recognizes those who have faith in Him as being righteous. A person can either trust that God will do the miracle of providing the righteousness needed to stand before Him, or a person can trust in his or her own way of dealing with this. Sadly, many people find themselves in the latter category. They do not trust God to save them. They are instead trying to save themselves by their good works, but again, this defeats the whole idea of grace. The fact is, God is willing to freely grant His forgiveness and righteousness to anyone who will trust in Him for salvation. If I am helplessly drowning in the ocean, my only real hope is for someone to save me. I cannot save myself because my own efforts will ultimately be futile. But when the life preserver is thrown, I simply have to reach out and grab on for dear life. This is what God is calling people to do—to reach out and grab hold of the Savior, Jesus Christ, to call out to Him and cling to Him in faith.

Adopted into God's Family

In looking at all of this, there are really only two kinds of people: those who trust in God and those who trust in themselves. Those who trust in God recognize that they are guilty and helpless before God, and they turn to God by trusting in the forgiveness He provides by sending His Son to bear the punishment for sin. And when a person does this, he or she is adopted into the family of God.

Marissa Cope was adopted as a newborn because of her mom's circumstances and her pregnancy being unplanned. Her adoptive parents worked out an adoption so that she would not be aborted. She writes,

> When my brother carried me out in his 6-year-old arms, he presented me to my parents and said, "Isn't she pretty? Doesn't she look just like me?"
>
> For me, being adopted is a picture of God's total sovereign control over all of the specific details he lovingly orchestrates in our lives. Over time, I have come to recognize a theme in my life of what I call ridiculous grace.
>
> I'm talking about the times God intervenes in our lives in such flagrant, extreme ways. He interrupts the logical order of things, and turns everything upside down in the best way possible. He took me from being an unplanned pregnancy, to being a much-wanted "chosen child."
>
> And there's the gospel—things were going along one way, but God intervened, and changed everything, because he's God and he's good and sovereign.
>
> When God adopts us into his family, it's a picture of what Christ has done to come and save us and bring us to the Father. And when Christ, our elder brother, presents us to his Father he says, "Isn't she pretty, doesn't she look just like me?" The Father loves and accepts us because of what Christ has done on our behalf.[34]

---

[34] Marissa Cope, "The Ridiculous Grace of Adoption" (available at http://thegospelcoalition.org/blogs/tgc/2013/11/21/the-ridiculous-grace-of-adoption/; accessed April 2014).

Paul talks about spiritual adoption as well in Romans. The beginning of the eighth chapter starts with one of the most wonderful statements in all of Scripture, "So now there is no condemnation for those who belong to Christ Jesus" (Romans 8:1 NLT). Paul is speaking about people who have placed their trust in Christ Jesus, and he says that those who have done so will never be condemned, or judged as guilty, by God. He goes on to talk about the fact that those who are in Christ have been given the Spirit of Christ. He says that those who live by their own moral efforts cannot please God because they are not truly aligned with God. In contrast, those who have the Spirit are able to please God and will receive eternal life (Romans 8:6–11).

Paul clearly states that if one belongs to Christ, then that person has been given His Spirit. The Bible also refers to this as the Holy Spirit. Paul goes on to say that God's Spirit is what makes the fact of adoption as well as the awareness of adoption possible. He says, "So you have not received a spirit that makes you fearful slaves. Instead, you received God's Spirit when he adopted you as his own children. Now we call him, 'Abba, Father.' For his Spirit joins with our spirit to affirm that we are God's children" (Romans 8:15–16 NLT).

He says that God's Spirit gives His children the ability to have such a close and loving relationship with God that they cry out to Him as "Abba, Father." The term *Abba* is one I remember hearing when I worked with young children in an after-school program in a highly Jewish-populated area outside of Boston. There was one particular little Jewish boy, four or five years old, who obviously had great affection toward his father. When his dad would come to pick him up, his eyes would light up, and he would run to his father, shouting, "Abba! Abba!" This is an Aramaic word that is equivalent to the term *Daddy* or *Papa*, and it obviously carries a strong connotation of tenderness and love. Therefore, when Paul says that those who have God's Spirit call Him Abba, he is saying that they see God much as this little boy saw his father. They feel great warmth and closeness to God because they know Him personally and love Him deeply, and they know He loves them deeply as well. It is God's Spirit that brings this about in their hearts.

Paul goes on to say that those who are God's children will also inherit great things from God. Because they follow Christ, there will be a certain amount of suffering in a world that by and large does not accept Christ, but in the end, they will be glorified with Him. They, like Christ, will die but will rise again to eternal life with God (Romans 8:17–19).

A New Identity, a New Life

One other thing that is important to mention regarding spiritual adoption is to recognize that those who have the Spirit of God have a new way of living. Paul makes a strong point that those who have the Spirit are no longer to live in the old way. He states,

> Therefore, dear brothers and sisters, you have no obligation to do what your sinful nature urges you to do. For if you live by its dictates, you will die. But if through the power of the Spirit you put to death the deeds of your sinful nature, you will live. For all who are led by the Spirit of God are children of God. (Romans 8:12–14 NLT)

One must remember that those who live merely by their own moral efforts cannot please God. But a person who has the Spirit of God now lives by the power of the Spirit so that he or she is actually able to put to death the deeds of sinfulness. This means that he or she no longer lives for sin but through God's Spirit lives for God. In other words, a person who is a child of God has the Spirit of God, and the Spirit of God changes that person's way of life. Just as I reflect many of the qualities of the family I grew up in because of the relationship I had with my family, a child of God reflects the character of God because he has a relationship with Him. This does not mean that when one becomes a child of God one is automatically perfect, but it does mean that the more time one spends in the presence and under the guidance of one's Father, the more one will take on the characteristics of one's Father. There will be a family resemblance.

And so those who trust in God for salvation through Christ will not only escape the judgment of God but are also able to enjoy fellowship with Him as their Father: "Abba." The source of all relationships offers each of us a close, personal relationship with Him!

The Problem of Accepting Love but Not God

Those who see God as a loving God but do not enter into a relationship with Him by faith are not grasping the full picture, and this has tremendous consequences. If a person rejects a relationship with God, then he or she will remain as one who must face God as judge. It is true that God has shown Himself to be loving. However, those who want to be treated well by God but continue to live apart from a loving relationship with Him must realize that there are no grounds for assuming acceptance by God.

The question of our relationship to God, therefore, is of utmost importance. The God who gave life, who is perfect, who will judge, and who showed His love through the death of His Son is calling people to a relationship with Him. If one chooses to ignore this offer, one is making a decision to reject what is fundamentally important, what truly does matter most. Nothing could be more catastrophic than this! For society as a whole, rejecting God will continue to bring the moral chaos and emptiness of soul so rampant today. For each individual, rejecting God will mean remaining guilty before Him, having to face an eternal sentence of separation from Him. One cannot afford to ignore these matters.

CHAPTER 8

GOD'S PURPOSE STATEMENT

Many of us, especially parents, have had the experience of talking to a child who wants to know why something is the way it is. We try to give an answer, and the answer is followed by another, "Why?" This is followed by another answer, which is then followed by another, "Why?" This is quite an exasperating exercise, as those who have been through it can attest.

While we may not really think much about it, this sort of conversation exposes a very interesting characteristic of humans. It seems, for some reason, that all people like to know why things are the way they are, revealing an innate desire to know the purpose behind what they experience. This brings us back to where we began. People ask questions because they sense that certain things really do matter, and one of the most fundamental things that matters to people is why things are the way they are. In other words, humans think purpose is very important.

In relation to this, there are many who would question why God would do things in the way described in this book. It bothers some to consider the possibility of God arranging things in this manner. I believe one cause of people's resistance is related a misunderstanding of God's purpose. We in this culture are continually fed on the premise that humans are what matter most. But if God wanted to create a world solely for humans, surely it seems He would have created one in which there were no suffering or death. So why would God create a world like this one, where there is so much turmoil and misery? In fact, the problem of pain and suffering has led many people to abandon belief in God altogether because it does not seem to coincide with the world they experience. And I would have to agree that much of religion today has erred by misrepresenting God as one who exists to cater to human desires.

It simply does not make sense that a God who places humans above all else would have created a world such as this. Even if it is argued that it is the rebellion of mankind against God, not God Himself, that has brought in the evil and suffering humans face, the fact remains that God created this world knowing all of this would happen. It is impossible to believe that God created this world with human happiness as His ultimate goal. This philosophical perspective is logically unsustainable, unless one is willing to question God's goodness or His power, which is what some have chosen to do. But I believe that all of this can be reconciled by looking at what the writers of Scripture have to say about God's purpose behind everything.[35] And hopefully it will be clear that everything discussed in this book concerning God and this life fits together seamlessly when seen through the lens of this purpose.

---

[35] Christians do have various views on how to solve the issue of why God made a world such as this. My approach here is to outline what the Bible teaches as best I can.

Why God Created the World

God Wanted to Show Himself

The first premise I would like to set forth is that God wanted to show Himself. He wanted to be seen. One of the ideas given so clearly in the Bible is that God has revealed Himself in a tremendous manner through the creation of this world. This is what the Psalmist alludes to when he says, "The heavens are telling of the glory of God; And their expanse is declaring the work of His hands" (Psalm 19:1 NASB). The physical universe, therefore, is a means by which God has enabled His person and glory to be manifested. He not only created physical objects that show forth His power, creativity, and beauty, but He also created beings that are able to perceive the greatness of His work.

However, even though God has shown Himself through the creation, this does not mean we are able to see God directly, in a physical sense. The Bible teaches that has invisible attributes, which can be observed in creation (Romans 1:20). In the book of John, Jesus said, "God is Spirit," and the beginning of this same book says no one has ever seen God (John 4:24, 1:18). Therefore, it is clear that in one sense God is invisible and we cannot see Him. However, not only does the creation show who He is, but Jesus, as we have already looked at, is the physical manifestation of God in human form. So God created a world in which to reveal Himself.

God Wanted to Be Seen for All That He Is

If God merely wanted to show Himself, then why bring a world into existence that contains evil?

The answer indicated in the Bible is that God has not only created a world to reveal Himself, but He has brought forth a world in which He is able to show the full array of His attributes. Though it is difficult to live in a world that has pain, it allows God's compassion to be demonstrated. And though it is troubling to deal with loss in life, this provides the opportunity for sacrifice to be made. This world exists in such a way that facets of God's character are displayed that could otherwise not be seen or understood.

This idea is evident in the stories we all know and love. A common characteristic of all of these stories is that they contain a bad situation. One of the most popular book and movie franchises of our time, *The Lord of the Rings*, certainly contains much that could be described as evil, and yet people never seem to take issue with the bad situations. They do not chide Tolkien for authoring a tale with all kinds of nasty creatures, perilous encounters, and evil forces at work. In fact, readers actually relish the inclusion of dire circumstances brought about by the presence of evil because it gives the opportunity for experientially profound qualities to be personified (whether it be love, courage, nobility, or sacrifice) that could never have been demonstrated otherwise. These experiences are part of what people treasure about the story, and the qualities revealed are ultimately what people love about the characters. In a parallel sense, the only way for God to show His love and power and perfection and justice, for humans to experience these things, and for God to be loved for these qualities, is in a world where evil and opposition exist. Without the evil, it is not possible to fully comprehend or enjoy the good. All great authors utilize this fact.

In the reality of life, God's many attributes can only be seen in their full glory against the backdrop of a world infested with evil. An important clarification is that what is evil originates in those who rebel against the goodness of God, not from God Himself. God is not the perpetrator of what is evil, but He has allowed the manifestation of evil to come about in order to show the greatness and splendor of who He is. Therefore, a world suffering the effects of evil, or sin, is actually the means by which God is able to demonstrate His love and grace, the culmination of which is seen at the cross where God Himself suffered on behalf of His enemies. Jesus Himself states, "God loved the world in this way: He gave His One and Only Son, so that everyone who believes in Him will not perish but have eternal life" (John 3:16 HCSB).

This is a demonstration of love that is hard to imagine—a Father giving up His Son to be killed in order to save those who were against Him, and a Son obediently laying down His life on behalf of those who deserve death. The only way in which this astounding love could be revealed is, though, was in a world that was suffering the effects of evil.

God Wanted to Be Known and Worshipped

According to Scripture, God's intention in all of this is not only to show His love toward His enemies, which is amazing in itself, but to bring those enemies to His side, which is exactly what is accomplished when He saves and adopts people into His family. Ultimately, God wanted to be known and worshipped, and the creation of this world has accomplished this purpose. People all over the world have seen the greatness and the love of God, and many have been adopted into His family and now know Him personally and worship Him with their lives.

But the ultimate climax of the worship of God is yet to come, when everything God has created and the purpose He has accomplished is fulfilled when the world as we know it comes to an end (and the world to come begins). This brings us to an extremely important concept revealed in Scripture, which is that ultimately those who have been forgiven of their sins will live forever with

God in a new heaven and a new earth, and those who do not turn to God in faith will face eternal punishment.[36] Eternity will fully demonstrate the power and glory of who God is, and He will be exalted and glorified above all else.

God will be glorified through the existence of heaven, where those who have experienced His grace and mercy will eternally live with Him and worship Him. Earlier in this book, I talked about the death of my brother-in-law, Scott. Scott was a believer in Jesus Christ, and he is in the presence of God today because God saved him from his sin and adopted him into His family. When Scott died, one of my relatives questioned why God would take the life of a young man who was just about to embark on a life of marriage and having a family. I would admit that it is hard to accept if one thinks of humans as being most important in this world, but if one accepts that God is most important—He is the one telling His story through creation—then individual human death can be seen from a different perspective. For the truth is, Scott is now in the greatest place imaginable, and because of Scott's death, many have learned about his faith in Christ and how they too can have a relationship with God. All of this is used by God to bring others to Himself so they can be with Him just as Scott is. So in the end, God has been glorified through all of this. This, of course does not answer all questions, but it gives a glimpse into the greater purposes of God.

But just as God is glorified through heaven, God will also be glorified through hell. God will demonstrate His wrath against those who are in opposition to Him. His justice will be shown, and His awesome holiness will be magnified as His enemies are punished in what the Bible calls the lake of fire. It is noteworthy how difficult

---

[36] Christians have different takes on what this will be like, but all Christians who believe the Bible agree that the two options that await all people are eternal life or God's judgment.

all of this is for humans to accept, which only uncovers their natural tendency not to see God as most important. People often bristle at the idea of God punishing sin, but what does this reveal? It shows that humans tend to think of humanity as more important than God Himself. If God is supreme and wants to show both His grace and holy justice in eternity, He has the ability and unique right to do so. Those who are opposed to this are revealing the basis of their own guilt—they refuse to acknowledge God's right to be God.

The points I am expressing here, again, are an echo of Paul's message in Romans. In chapter 9 he states,

> And what if God, desiring to display His wrath and to make His power known, endured with much patience objects of wrath ready for destruction? And what if He did this to make known the riches of His glory on objects of mercy that He prepared beforehand for glory? (Romans 9:22–23 HCSB)

Paul is raising the point that God is willing to endure the rebellion of those who will ultimately face destruction in order to show His wrath and His power, and He is using the presence of evil to demonstrate His grace to those who have received His mercy. People in this passage are described as being either prepared for destruction or prepared for glory. In other words, God purposely made them ultimately knowing each person's destiny—some would be punished and some would be saved in order to show the glory of who He is.

This, as I said before, is difficult to accept, and it is at this point that we are tempted to ask, "Why would God create people whom He knew would be eternally punished?" Paul anticipates this kind of question, and the answer is: God can do what He wants because

He is God (Romans 9:20). He has the right and the power to do what He wants with what He has made, and if He wants to show His wrath, power, and grace by creating a world such as this, then He has the right and ability to do so, and this is exactly what He has done. He is God, and we are not.

Jesus' Take on What Really Matters

Embracing the purpose of God, then, rises or falls on being able to accept God's unique position and prerogative. Many people mistakenly see God as unjust because if a human did what God did, that human would be unjust. God, however, is not a human. He is not our equal. He, as Creator, Giver of life, and the perfect, holy Judge, has a unique prerogative and right over His creation. He stands over humanity, not vice versa. Even heaven and hell are a testimony to His supreme place in the universe.

In contrast to everything I have portrayed in this book, people often choose to live under the notion that their lives are important apart from God. I believe this is an empty philosophy because, in the end, no matter what success they may achieve, all will be lost the moment they die. They may think that their possessions and personal achievements are the marks of a life well-lived, but this is merely wishful thinking negated by one reality: death is immanent, and all of the things that have been gained and achieved will come to nothing. Jesus' question strikes at the heart of this issue, "What will it profit a man if he gains the whole world, and loses his own soul?" (Mark 8:36 NKJV). And consider the story He tells.

> "A rich man's land was very productive. He thought
> to himself, 'What should I do, since I don't have

anywhere to store my crops? I will do this,' he said. 'I'll tear down my barns and build bigger ones and store all my grain and my goods there. Then I'll say to myself, 'You[e] have many goods stored up for many years. Take it easy; eat, drink, and enjoy yourself.'

"But God said to him, 'You fool! This very night your life is demanded of you. And the things you have prepared—whose will they be?'

"That's how it is with the one who stores up treasure for himself and is not rich toward God." (Luke 12:16–21 HCSB)

The truth is, no matter how much one achieves, the only thing that ultimately matters is a life lived in relation to God. If a person denies the importance of God and lives for himself, he will lose everything in the end, including his own soul. However, if a person realizes and accepts the reality that God is most important, then he is on the brink of fulfilling the true purpose of life—worshipping God—and he will be living for what truly matters.

PART 3

LIVING
FOR WHAT
MATTERS MOST

CHAPTER 9

FIRST THINGS FIRST

Throughout the course of this book, I have been seeking to show how human experience points to the reality and importance of God. The last chapter argued that God's whole purpose in making everything was to show forth and declare the glory of who He is. If this premise is correct, it should follow that the responsibility God has given and communicated to mankind should line up with this purpose. If a teacher, for example, has the goal of giving her students the best education possible, then she will expect and tell her students to listen and study because that is the only way they will reach the goal of getting a good education. So if it is God's goal to be glorified and worshipped above all else, then it would make sense for Him to give instructions that would coincide with this goal.

The biblical author Matthew tells of a man who came to Jesus and asked Him what the most important command in the law was. This man was a Jew, and the law to which he referred is the series of books commonly referred to as the Old Testament. In these books, many of the commands of God are given, and in an attempt to trap

Jesus in His own words, this man asked Jesus what seemed to be a very difficult question. Perhaps he wanted to see which religious sect Jesus' answer would favor and thus back Him into a corner and force Him to take sides. But Jesus silenced His opponents with an answer that transcended any arguments and divisions they may have had.

> Jesus said to him, "'You shall love the LORD your God with all your heart, with all your soul, and with all your mind.'" (Matthew 22:37 NKJV)

Jesus was quoting from an Old Testament passage found in Deuteronomy 6:5. According to Jesus, out of all the commands given in Scripture, the most important one is to love God above all else. This clearly coincides with God's purpose of being worshipped above all else, for it is the primary thing He expects of humanity, as seen from Jesus' response.

It is important to note that not only does God command that people love Him; God also deserves love. Remember, He is the source of all existence, and if one enjoys or values anything or anyone, it is ultimately owed to God's creative activity. Therefore, when God commands that people love Him, it is partly because His ultimate goal is to be glorified and worshipped above everything, but it is also because He deserves to be glorified and worshipped above everything. Many people's complaints concerning God would be assuaged by recognizing His unique status as God. Parents should be valued for providing for their children. A president should be honored for his elected position. And God should be worshipped and honored because He is the Creator, Sustainer, and Provider of everything.

Now there are those who are bothered by the concept of God placing Himself above all others and expecting the love of humans;

some feel this kind of God sounds like a megalomaniac. Two things must be observed, however. First of all, if God were to put someone else above Himself, it would certainly not be a good thing. The truth is, if He put any person above all else and did whatever that particular person thought would make him or her happy at any given moment, the end result would be disaster for everyone, including the person God put above everything else. Even in pop culture, the movie *Bruce Almighty* explores this theme and concludes that God has much more to be concerned with than the wishes and perspective of one person.

This leads to a second observation: God is actually showing the greatest love for humanity by putting Himself first. The paradox is that He gave up the most important thing He could have given (His own Son) to show His love. Therefore in one sense, He was putting humanity above Himself in the way He sacrificed. He showed humility in doing this. However, His ultimate goal in doing this was to bring glory to Himself (Philippians 2:5–11). His glory brings His joy. And while His glorification is satisfying to Him, it is ultimately the pathway to human happiness as well. God, through His purposes, has given people the means by which to experience the greatest happiness, and that happiness is found in the God who is joyful because He possesses what He desires and deserves: the honor, glory, and worship of His creation.

God's call to love Him, then, is not selfish on His part. It is a call to embark on a relationship of soul satisfaction. The invitation to love God is like the invitation to a parched person in a desert to come to an oasis and drink. Therefore, it is actually for the good and joy of humanity that God would place Himself above all and expect their love. This is one reason why the message of Jesus is called the gospel—good news!

What This Command Means

Because God is of ultimate importance and the most important responsibility is to love Him, what does this look like in everyday, real life?

First of all, one should note that this command is not dependent on the defense of a particular religious group. It is true, unfortunately, that many people have had bad experiences associated with religion, and it has turned them off to the idea of pursuing God altogether. I have personally seen people conned, used, and hurt in the name of religion, and it is a tragedy. However, to abandon the pursuit of God is to neglect the ultimate purpose of life, which is not worth relinquishing because of negative experiences. Anyhow, Jesus' statement reveals the fundamental issue is not religious affiliation per se but loving God above all else, about having relationship with Him. This relationship is entered into through faith in Jesus and being adopted into God's family. The truth is that even people who are heavily involved with religion may be missing the fundamentally important trait of love toward God. Even some of the people Jesus was addressing when He stated this command, though religious, did not truly love God. This not only reveals inadequacy of religion itself to produce what is most important spiritually but also the reason why people who are religious can give it a bad name. The first command is to love God, not to become religious.

On the other hand, even though religious affiliation itself is not the focus of this command, one must not conclude that a person can show love to God in whatever way one pleases. Everyone knows, I should hope, that the only way in which to show love for others is to learn about them in a personal way and strive to do the things that please them according to their personal likes and dislikes. If I want to show love to my wife, in my case, I have learned not to spend a great amount of money on her for her birthday but to give her a card and a modest, practical gift. While it may be the case that many women like to receive expensive and extravagant presents, like jewelry with a big bouquet of roses, if I were to buy my wife these things for her birthday, the end result would be miserable for both of us. My wife likes to see money spent on useful things, even on her birthday. (That is why I bought her a chainsaw for her birthday several years ago; in her eyes, it was a very romantic thing to do.) Therefore, showing love toward my wife means doing things according to the way she likes them, not the way I or someone else thinks she ought to like them.

Sadly, many people miss this point in relation to God. Instead, they often concoct an image of God with their own imagination and then show love to Him in the way they think God ought to like. Imagine a man who wants to date a woman, imagines what she is like based on a picture he has seen, and determines how to treat her based on his private notions rather than correspondence with her. When he goes out with the actual woman (not the version in his head), he does things she does not like (taking her to a romantic movie when she actually likes action movies). And whenever she tries to tell him how she really feels about different things, he interrupts her and says he would rather love her according to how he has imagined her. Aside from having a ludicrous view of relationships (and perhaps some need for psychological medical attention), a man like this does not actually have true love for this woman. Those who approach God in this manner are not showing true love toward Him either, regardless of how much effort they are putting into it.

Therefore, in order to truly love God, one must seek to know Him, and one will learn who He truly is by reading what He has disclosed about Himself in Scripture (2 Timothy 3:16–17). When I first met my wife, we were in college, and during the summer, she went home to New Hampshire, and I went home to New Jersey. Even though we were hundreds of miles apart, we still communicated with each other through writing letters. We learned a lot about one another, coming know each other in an even deeper way as we expressed our thoughts on paper. God also has expressed Himself on paper, and it is possible to know Him in the most intimate of ways by reading His communication to us.

It is good that God has given us written communication because it provides an objective way for people to understand who He is. This is important because it is possible to be deceived about spiritual matters. There are many different messages being touted, and the best thing for any person to do is to begin to study the Bible to see what God has disclosed. As one does this, one will begin to see that God has a specific way He is bringing people into His family and uniting them together to worship and bring glory to His name. This group in Scripture is called the church. I will not get into the details of all that is involved regarding the church, but the important thing to see at this point is that God has established the church, and those who desire to show love to Him are called to be involved with other believers as a part of the church.

My aim here, it should be noted, is not to promote a certain Christian denomination but to simply accept the reality that God has established a particular way in which He wants to be worshipped and in which to carry out His plan. One needs merely to take a cursory look at Scripture to see that this is so. And if one is going to truly carry out the command to love God, then one must do things in the way that pleases Him according to His liking.

In regard to church and what is often called organized religion, I realize that many people feel frustrated because religion seems fraught with hypocrisy and divisions, and popular books, such as Christopher Hitchens subtly titled *God Is Not Great: How Religion*

Poisons Everything, reinforce a negative image of any sort of organized religion. But a few things must be said about this. First, even if there are many problems with religion, this does not give one an excuse to abandon it altogether, for the concept of church (the gathering of God's people in an organized manner) is God's appointed means of being worshipped. So if one wants to do things His way, one should take the idea of church seriously.

Second, it is also vital to remember that there are always going to be those who take a good thing and use it in the wrong way. There are those who run businesses and cheat their customers or employees, but this does not mean that "organized business" is a hopeless endeavor that ought to be abandoned altogether. Likewise, there are schools that are run poorly with students receiving a subpar education, but it would be foolish and tragic to completely give up on the use of educational institutions. Misuse of a good concept is no reason to do away with it entirely. It does mean, though, that one needs to approach the matter with a sense of discernment, realizing that not all religious institutions (i.e., churches) or religious followers (i.e., church members) are going to be what they claim to be. One must, based on the great commandment, search for a church that is characterized by a true love for God. It is also a reality that some readers, in order to make a fresh attempt at church, may need to forgive those who have misused religion.

Finally, in regard to the fact that there are so many different kinds of churches, this should not ultimately discourage a person from being involved. It is simply evidence of human fallibility and of the fact that there is no perfect church with perfect people. Neither are there perfect marriages, but marriage relationships are nonetheless still valuable. In spite of human imperfection, there are churches that are characterized by a true love for God, and the evidence for this is that they seek to know Him and follow what He has revealed in Scripture. These are the kinds of churches worth pursing involvement in.

Loving God with All the Heart, Soul, Mind, and Strength

So to love God, first of all, means to seek to know Him and honor Him in the way He desires. Second, the command that Jesus gives also shows the extent to which this love must go. The call is to love God with all of the heart, soul, mind, and strength.

Many people think of Christianity as being about attending service on Sunday and then trying to be a good person the rest of the week, but this command entails much more than just a surface incorporation of God in our lives. He is to be at the center of one's life. It seems that even many people who attend churches do not see Christianity in this way, and yet this is what Christianity was meant to be, according to Jesus. Anyone who takes the time to read through Scripture will see clearly that the entire Bible is really centered on God and His greatness. The people in the Bible were ordinary people who make mistakes just like all of us, but they worshipped a great God who accomplished great things in their lives. Regrettably, it is easy for churches to lose this focus, and the Scripture is made out to be a handbook on how to live the good life. Instead, it should be seen as a handbook on how to live the God-centered life, for everything in the Bible declares that God is worthy of supreme devotion.

A great example to me of the total abandon to God that should characterize one's life is observed in the Christian missionary team that went in the mid-1950s to minister to the Waodani people of Ecuador, an extremely violent tribe. The team's endeavor is depicted in the movie *The End of the Spear*. The five men who were part of the team were ultimately murdered by members of the tribe out of fear and distrust. But two women, Elizabeth Elliott and Rachel Saint, returned and continued to try to make inroads into understanding the tribal members and teach them about God. Their sacrificial and forgiving spirit ultimately led to the tribe's radical transformation from a culture of violence to one of peace. What brought all of this about was the God-centered and abandoned attitude of those who were willing to give everything to reach this people group. Their fully devoted mind-set is summed up in the words of Jim Elliott, who wrote in his journal, "He is no fool who gives what he cannot keep to gain that which he cannot lose." This perspective reveals what wholehearted love for God looks like. Not everyone is called to go serve a remote tribe of people, but all Christians are called to be fully surrendered to God's will.

Our Reasonable Service

By now it is no surprise that what I have been discussing is also reflected in Paul's presentation of Christianity in the book of Romans. At the end of the eleventh chapter, as he comes to a close on the subject of God's plan to bring people into a relationship to Himself through the power of the gospel, he utters these remarkable words:

Oh, the depth of the riches of the wisdom and knowledge of God!
How unsearchable his judgments,
and his paths beyond tracing out!
"Who has known the mind of the Lord?
Or who has been his counselor?"
"Who has ever given to God,
that God should repay them?"
For from him and through him and for him are all things.

To him be the glory forever! Amen. (Romans 11:33–36 NIV)

This passage magnifies the fact that everything is from God, everything belongs to God, everything is for God, and therefore, God is the greatest and most important thing in the universe (the major premise of this book). Then, in the next sentence, he goes on to state what the response of people should be in light of who God is and what He has done: "Therefore, I urge you, brothers and sisters, in view of God's mercy, to offer your bodies as a living sacrifice, holy and pleasing to God—this is your true and proper worship" (Romans 12:1 NIV).

Paul says that everything about God and His offer of salvation and relationship to people begs a response, and Paul passionately calls for this response. "Offer your bodies as a living sacrifice" is another way of saying, "Love the Lord with everything you are and have." People should respond to God in love and devotion because of His love and mercy. He has clearly demonstrated His mercy by providing a way for people to be forgiven of their sins and to have this relationship of love with Him through faith in Jesus. He deserves a response of love, and He has shown mercy to provide the way for people to know Him and be able to love Him. Therefore, Paul says, offer your bodies as a living sacrifice. Give your whole life to the one who deserves everything you have to give.

Finally, Paul says this response is our "true and proper worship," or a more literal translation of the original Greek, "our reasonable service." The priests who served God among the Jews in the days before Jesus came were performing a spiritual service to God. In the system that they were in, they would offer sacrifices to God as a spiritual act of worship. Here, Paul is saying that our spiritual service, our worship, should be to offer ourselves. This is the logical response in light of who God is and what He has done.

God Is Most Important

The first part of this book discussed the premise that God matters most. The second part of this book seeks to discover what this should mean for one's life. The resounding answer from Jesus and the writers of Scripture is to respond to God with wholehearted love and devotion, to be a living sacrifice for Him because He is the one who is worthy and has provided a means of living in right relationship to Him. In other words, because God is most important, one should live as though He is most important.

The opposite of this lifestyle of God-centeredness is a life of self-centeredness—the default mind-set of humanity. God meant for people to live for much more than themselves, and coming into a relationship with Him through faith in Christ changes one's perspective. A person who responds to God in faith can see and accept that life is really about Him. But it does not end here.

CHAPTER 10

LAST BUT NOT LEAST

Loving God is first, but Jesus goes on to give another command of utmost importance: "Love your neighbor as yourself" (Matthew 22:39). A man once asked a Christian college professor how one can really display love toward God, since God has no needs. The professor's response was that love toward God is shown by meeting the needs of others, as revealed in Jesus' statement "to the extent that you did it to one of these brothers of Mine, even the least of them, you did it to Me." The professor writes, "When you love people in Jesus' name, you are loving Jesus. When those who are precious to Jesus become precious to you, you are loving God with all of your heart, soul, and mind."[37]

The second command, therefore, is actually the natural complement and outflow of the first command, not an arbitrary addition. It is actually a means of obeying the first command, for

---

[37] W. Oscar Thompson, *Concentric Circles of Concern: Seven Stages for Making Disciples* (Nashville, TN: Broadman and Holman Publishers, 1999), 152–153.

God wants people to show love to Him *by* showing love to others. And showing love to others out of love for God brings glory to Him, thus fulfilling the first command. This is because loving others in the way that Jesus speaks of is really about showing the character of God, demonstrating His likeness so others are able to see the goodness of God through His people. Jesus said, "Let your light so shine before men, that they may see your good works and glorify your Father in heaven" (Matthew 5:16 NKJV). Jesus did this very thing by caring for the needs of others and pointing them to God, and He calls His followers to do the same.

And when Christians truly live this out, it is a powerful testimony of God's love. Ravi Zacharias, quoting Marie Chapian, provides a moving example of this. It is the story of a Christian named Yakov who is telling an older man named Cimmerman about Christ.

> When Yakov talked to him about the love of Christ, Cimmerman said, "Don't talk to me about Christ! You see those priests there, with all their vestments, all of their cloaks, all of the big crosses on their chests? I know what they're like. They're violent people. They have abused their power. Don't tell me about Christ! I know what it is to watch them kill our people, even some of my own relatives."
>
> Yakov paused for a moment and then said, "Cimmerman, can I ask you a question? What if I stole your cloak and your boots, put them on, broke into a bank and took the money? I was chased by the police but I outran them. What would you say if the police came knocking on your door and charged you with breaking into a bank?"

Cimmerman said, "I would deny it because I did not."

"Ah! But what if they say that they recognized your coat and your boots from a distance? You had to have broken into the bank!"

Cimmerman said, "Yakov, just leave me alone. I know what you're driving at. I do not want to get into this discussion."

Yakov went away, but he kept coming back only to live the love of Christ before him. Finally one day Cimmerman said, "Yakov, tell me about this Christ that you so love and live for. How can I know him?" Yakov told him how to commit his life to Christ. Cimmerman knelt down on the dust outside his home with Yakov and received Christ into his life. He stood up and embraced Yakov and said, "Thank you for being in my life. You wear his coat very well."[38]

When people see the love of Christ through His people, God's likeness is demonstrated and He is glorified. Thus, loving others is a means of fulfilling the first command.

Human Love versus God's Love

The second command is also seen to flow from the first in that loving God provides the groundwork for truly loving others—the

---

[38]   Ravi Zacharias, *Telling the Truth: Evangelizing Postmoderns*, (Grand Rapids, MI: Zondervan, 2000), 42.

reason being that God is the source of true and pure love, and without God, humans do not naturally love each other as they ought. People may be loving in one sense, but it is different than the love of which Christ speaks.

One way this can be seen is in people's determination of whom they will love. Typically people will love certain individuals but not others. The people they love may be family and friends, and there are usually reasons for loving these people that are based on something about the other person. I may love and care about someone because he is such a good friend or because she is my daughter or because he has done so much for our family and so on. People tend to believe they have a right to love others based on how others relate to them. So if a person doesn't respect me, then I should not have to love him or her, or so the thinking goes.

Jesus, on the other hand, tells His followers, "Love your enemies... and pray for those who spitefully use you and persecute you" (Matthew 5:44 NKJV). Jesus says that loving only those who are good to you is natural and is no indication that you are showing any moral greatness. Even the most obviously immoral people can show kindness to others who cater to their own desires. The worst criminal may be kind and even love those who will tell him and give him what he wants. This, then, is one indication of how people showing love apart from loving God falls short of the true love commanded by Jesus.

Another way people's love is shown to fall short of the love described by Jesus is in the goal it has for the person who is the object of love. Most people's love, even at its best, is not aimed at the highest good of the other person. Seeking to make others happy by meeting their physical needs or by befriending them is a noble task, but it falls short of meeting their greatest need. Without God, they will still be left apart from the joy of knowing and loving the giver of life, the source of true goodness, and the one who can provide freedom from the power of sin in this life and from the punishment of sin in the life to come. Therefore even the most loving person who does not love God first is only aiming at bringing others temporary happiness, and this falls short of the love that aims at the deep-rooted joy and eternal happiness of a relationship with God.

The only way to love others rightly, then, is to put God first. Doing so frees one to love selflessly and with an aim toward the highest good of others. It also allows one to see people as of inherent value and that they ought to be regarded with dignity and care. When God is removed from the equation, people can be viewed as mere products of a natural world, just more life forms taking up limited resources. This is a logical outflow of the theory that life arose apart from God and leads to some very important ethical questions. How is one to think of the countless people in our world? Are they expendable based on their contribution to humanity, or ought life to be protected? Are the needs of others around the world as significant as the pursuit of one's own lifestyle of comfort and wealth? A person's perspective about God can have tremendous implications for one's valuing of and responsibility toward others.

How to Love Others

So loving others rightly comes out of loving God first, but how exactly does one carry this out? One clue is found within the command. It tells us to love our neighbor as we love ourselves. In what ways do people show love to themselves? They take care of themselves, they think about themselves, and they try to fulfill themselves. Therefore, Jesus teaches that one should do the same for others—think about them, take care of them, and seek to fulfill them. In essence, people should be doing to others what they would want others to do for them.

Jesus was once having a discussion with a man about the two great commands. The man knew that the greatest commands and ultimate point of Scripture was for people to love God supremely and love others as they love themselves. But as the man thought about the command to love his neighbor, he started to sense that he wasn't really showing the kind of love that God wants. He realized that his love was limited and biased, and he began to internally squirm a bit, so he asked Jesus, "Who is my neighbor?" Jesus responded with this story:

> "A Jewish man was traveling from Jerusalem down to Jericho, and he was attacked by bandits. They stripped him of his clothes, beat him up, and left him half dead beside the road.
>
> "By chance a priest came along. But when he saw the man lying there, he crossed to the other side of the road and passed him by. A Temple assistant walked over and looked at him lying there, but he also passed by on the other side.
>
> "Then a despised Samaritan came along, and when he saw the man, he felt compassion for him. Going over to him, the Samaritan soothed his wounds with olive oil and wine and bandaged them. Then he put the man on his own donkey and took him to an inn, where he took care of him. The next day he handed the innkeeper two silver coins, telling him, 'Take care of this man. If his bill runs higher than this, I'll pay you the next time I'm here.'" (Luke 10:30–35 NLT)

There are some very important things to learn about love for others through Jesus' illustration. First of all, Jesus shows that one's love for others should be unconditional. This is one of the main points of Jesus' story because the man who showed love was a Samaritan, and Samaritans were enemies of the Jews. It would be equivalent in our day to saying that a Palestinian took a Jew under his wing when he saw that the Jew was in need of medical attention. Jesus gives a penetrating and indicting contrast to this in portraying two Jews, a priest and a temple assistant, who were unwilling to help. The ones who were fellow countrymen, who were very respectable in that culture, would not intervene. But the enemy of the Jew, the one disdained in this culture, ended up showing true love.

Such a tremendous lesson can be learned in this. The love one shows to others should not be limited to people who are of a certain race or religion. It saddens me to hear the negative comments people often make about those from other countries. This is not to say that there are not legitimate problems with other countries, just as there are legitimate problems with America, but I often hear the attitude of the man Jesus spoke with coming out in the opinions given about people of certain ethnicities or religious backgrounds. They do not see these people as neighbors who ought to be loved. Rather, they see these people as part of a country that endorses evil things, and therefore they are unworthy of love. And the same attitude often prevails even within the border of this country as well. People in one religious group do not have love for people within another religious group, and people associated with one political party do not love those associated with another political party.

Now I am not saying there are no good reasons for division among people any more than Jesus was saying that the Jews and the Samaritans have no significant points of difference. In fact, Jesus told a Samaritan woman that salvation is of the Jews (cf. John

4:22). The Jews were the ones who had the message of truth (in the Scriptures) and the Messiah (which is Jesus) who would bring salvation to the people of the world. The Samaritans were off in their beliefs, and Jesus said so, but this did not negate the fact that both the Jews and the Samaritans still had an obligation to love each other even in the midst of their differing beliefs. The Samaritan in Jesus' story illustrates the necessity of showing love to all people without condition, whether they are white, black, Asian, Latino, Catholic, Protestant, liberal, conservative, Buddhist, Muslim, tall, short, fat, thin, cultured, uncultured, nice, or mean. It doesn't matter. Jesus' call is to show love to all people in the same way we love ourselves without regard to our own unique qualities as a person.

Another lesson in this story is that true love reveals itself in tangible, need-meeting ways. It is not enough just to talk about love; there must also be a willingness to do something for others. The Samaritan didn't just feel bad for the man lying on the side of the road; he did not just complain about the social evils of the culture; he actually helped him. He gave him his time and a ride to a town, and he paid for the man to stay in a place where he could recuperate. Our love should be seen in what we do for others, just as we would do more than feel sorry for ourselves if we were cold and hungry. We would actually do something to meet our own needs—we would put on a coat; we would get some food. Love should actually meet the needs of others.

The third thing about love in this story is that it is sacrificial. Not only did the Samaritan do something to help out, but he also did something at a cost to himself. He may have had a lot to do that day, but he gave up a great amount of time and spent money out of his own pocket for a complete stranger. We Americans especially need to examine ourselves in this area because we have so much, but what are we really willing to give even though there are so many needs out there? There is so much we could give to show love, especially if we were truly willing to sacrifice. It would move us deeply and bring great joy if someone sacrificed on our behalf, and if we were to love others as we love ourselves, we would sacrifice for them.

Author Rebecca Pippert tells a story about a young nurse that sums up Jesus' portrayal of love. She was caring for a woman named Eileen who had experienced a debilitating cerebral aneurysm.

As near as the doctors could tell Eileen was totally unconscious, unable to feel pain and unaware of anything going on around her... As a result, more and more she came to be treated as a thing, a vegetable, and the hospital jokes about her room—room 415—were gross and dehumanizing.

But the young student nurse decided that she could not treat this person like the others had treated her. She talked to Eileen, sang to her, encouraged her, and even brought her little gifts. One day when things were especially difficult and it would have been easy for the young nurse to take out her frustrations on the patient, she was especially kind. It was Thanksgiving Day and the nurse said to the patient, "I was in a cruddy mood this morning, Eileen, because it was supposed to be my day off. But now that I'm here, I'm glad. I wouldn't have wanted to miss seeing you on Thanksgiving. Do you know this is Thanksgiving?"

Just then the telephone rang, and as the nurse turned to answer it, she looked quickly back at Eileen. "Suddenly," she writes, Eileen was "looking at me… crying. Big damp circles stained her pillow, and she was shaking all over."

That was the only human emotion that Eileen ever showed any of them, but it was enough to change the whole attitude of the hospital staff toward her. Not long afterward, Eileen died. The young nurse closes her story, saying, "I keep thinking about her… It occurred to me that I owe her an awful lot. Except for Eileen, I might never have known what it's like to give myself to someone who can't give back"[39]

What a tremendous example of the reality and power of the unconditional, tangible, sacrificial love to which Jesus call us!

The Goal of This Love

Jesus' story of the Good Samaritan and the story about the nurse are both moving illustrations of love, but in these stories it is easy to overlook an important aspect of love. If it is seen as merely doing nice things for others, then the heart of what God's love is really about is being missed altogether. One must remember to view love in light of the command to love God above all else.

Jesus does not merely want people to do good to others; He wants them to do good as a means of glorifying God, helping others to see who He is. When a person shows love in an unconditional, tangible, sacrificial way, this lifestyle manifests the very kind of love

---

[39]   Rebecca Pippert, *Out of the Salt Shaker and into the World* (Downers Grove: Intervarsity Press, 1979), 110–11.

that God showed in sending His Son to bear the punishment for sin. God gave His Son for people who were in rebellion against Him (unconditional love); He gave His Son who was a physical person who physically reached out to the world and physically was tortured and killed (tangible love); and He gave His only Son (the only Son who comes from God Himself), whom He loved and adored, in order to bear the sin of the world (sacrificial love). As one shows God's likeness through unconditional, tangible, sacrificial love, that person then has a viable platform from which to speak of God's righteousness, love, and grace to people who do not know Him.

In contrast, taking the ultimate aim of glorifying God out of the equation distorts what it means to truly love others. People may claim that it is unloving not to affirm another person's lifestyle choices. However, if one sees love in connection with leading people to God, then love may not always affirm what others do. It seeks change in others for a higher good. On a physical level, it may seem loving to allow a person to overeat all of the time—to let him do whatever makes him happy. If, on the other hand, a concerned friend confronts that person about the long-term effects of his eating habits, that person may not feel loved. In reality, though, the friend is acting at a higher level of love in seeking the long-term health of the overeater. Jesus Himself confronted people regularly (both the religious and nonreligious) out of concern for their ultimate well-being. This is true love, and this is the love Jesus calls us to emulate.

Therefore, the most loving thing one can do is to show the goodness of God to others while also caringly exposing the things that are ultimately hurting them and showing them how they can find forgiveness and grace to change. And if they turn to Christ for forgiveness and change, then they will be able to love God in a personal relationship, will be set free to love others selflessly, and will glorify God as they demonstrate His likeness. This lifestyle will lead more and more people to God, allowing His love to continually spread as people come to know Him and live out His love. In all of this, He will be worshipped and loved and honored as the one who is the source of all that matters in life.

And so it is fitting to conclude with the words of Paul: "Owe no one anything except to love one another, for he who loves another has fulfilled the law" (Romans 13:8 NKJV). Love God and love others for His glory. May we live to this end, for this is living for what matters most!